Twayne's English Authors Series

Sylvia E. Bowman, *Editor*

INDIANA UNIVERSITY

Ælfric

TEAS 131

Ælfric

By JAMES HURT
University of Illinois

Twayne Publishers, Inc. :: New York

Library of Congress Catalog Card Number: 76–162871

MANUFACTURED IN THE UNITED STATES OF AMERICA

Preface

The inclusion of Ælfric in the Twayne English Authors Series might suggest a number of perennial questions about the continuity of English literature and the propriety of maintaining or not maintaining the great gulf that ordinarily separates Old English and later literature. These questions certainly deserve the attention they have received, but I have chosen to ignore them in this brief study of the most accomplished prose writer of the Old English period. I have taken for granted that Ælfric and his works are worth studying for their own sake and that they deserve the attention of anyone interested in good writing, whether he is especially interested in Old English or not.

I do not minimize, however, the problems that confront the nonspecialist in approaching the work of a writer so remote from us chronologically and, in some ways, intellectually. I have therefore attempted in the first chapter not only to summarize what is known of Ælfric's life but also to suggest something of his social, political, and intellectual environment. The brevity and superficiality of this survey may offend the specialist, but I have chosen to risk doing so rather than to puzzle other readers by omitting all mention of the conditions which inspired Ælfric's work and guided its course.

In the succeeding chapters, rather than following an all-inclusive, chronological plan, I have selected five aspects of Ælfric's achievement and organized each chapter around one of these topics. Chapter 2 deals with Ælfric as a homilist; Chapter 3, with his work as a hagiographer; Chapter 4, with his Bible translations; and Chapter 5, with his pedagogical texts for Latin instruction. The final chapter abandons this organization by content to consider Ælfric's prose style, the aspect of his work for which he is chiefly remembered.

The problem of quotations has been difficult. It seems very important that such a stylist not be quoted in inevitably lame modern translation, but I realized also that many readers lack a knowledge of Old English. I have therefore quoted Ælfric in Old

English but have included a modern translation immediately following each quotation. These have been included in the text, rather than in the notes, as a matter of the reader's convenience. The translations are for the most part my own, rather than published translations, because I believed it desirable that the modern translations be genuinely modern and reasonably consistent in style. Ælfric's Latin is quoted only in English (S.H. Gem's translations). Although Ælfric's Latin style deserves more attention, I have not considered it necessary to include the Latin texts here.

The texts of the quotations are drawn from the standard editions cited in the Bibliography. Here again I have striven for clarity and consistency. In general, I have followed the principles presented by John Pope in his valuable new edition of the previously unedited homilies. That is, although the "ordinary prose" is printed in the customary way, passages in "rhythmical prose" are arranged in rhythmical lines, whether they are so arranged in the printed texts or not. There are, however, no medial spaces between "half-lines." This method should call attention to the form without suggesting that it is poetic in any sense and should aid the reader in perceiving the correct rhythm. All punctuation has been altered, if necessary, from the printed texts to conform with modern practice, again to make it easier to read the texts easily and accurately. No indications of stress or length have been included, and certain symbols have been silently expanded. (The Old English ampersand, for instance, has always been expanded to "and.") References are identified in the text, rather than the footnotes. The abbreviations are, I believe, self-explanatory, and always refer to the printed texts listed in the Bibliography.

James Hurt

University of Illinois

Contents

Chronology

c. 955	Ælfric born, probably somewhere in Wessex.
c. 970	Entered the Old Monastery at Winchester.
c. 985	Ordained as a priest.
987	Went to the newly founded monastery at Cernel.
989	*Catholic Homilies* I.
992	*Catholic Homilies* II.
992–1002	*De Temporibus Anni, Grammar, Glossary, Genesis, Colloquy, Interrogationes, De Falsis Deis, De XII Abusivis, Lives of Saints, Hexameron, Joshua* (in approximately this order, along with miscellaneous other homilies and occasional pieces).
1002–1005	*Numbers, Judges, Admonitio* (probably also a series of forty homilies for the Proper of the Season, called by Clemoes Temporale Homilies I).
1005	Went to the new monastery of Eynsham as abbot; Latin *Letters for Wulfstan; Letter to the Monks of Eynsham.*
1005–c. 1010	*Letter to Sigeweard,* reissue of *Catholic Homilies* I, *Life of Æthelwold,* English *Letters for Wulfstan,* probably another series of homilies (Temporale Homilies II), reissue of *Catholic Homilies* II.
c. 1010	Ælfric died.

CHAPTER 1

Ælfric and the Tenth Century

ABBOT Ælfric of Eynsham was born about the middle of the tenth century, and his life spanned the last half of that century, a period of great political, social, and intellectual activity. He saw during his lifetime a renaissance of English culture that rivaled and in some ways surpassed the earlier "golden age" of intellectual and artistic activity in eighth-century Northumbria. He also lived to see what England had dreaded above all else, the renewal of attacks by the Danes, whose depredations during the preceding century had been halted by King Alfred. They descended again during his lifetime, "like wolves," Ælfric said, and threw England into a political and economic chaos ended only by the conquest of the island by William the Conqueror, several decades after Ælfric's death.

Ælfric's life and work were intimately related to his age. He led a quiet life and participated, as far as we know, in none of the great political events of his time. We do not know how well known he was during his own lifetime, but in retrospect, it seems that his work so well reflects the quality of his age that we may speak of the late tenth century as the Age of Ælfric, as we speak of the eighth century as the Age of Bede or the ninth century as the Age of Alfred.

I *England 950–1000*

The birth of Ælfric at mid-century happened to coincide with the end of a long and tortuous process of political reunification of England after the assaults of the Danes in the ninth century.[1] The Danes had attacked Lindisfarne in 793; over the first half of the ninth century, their incursions grew in size and ferocity until it was clear by 850 that they intended to conquer the whole island. In 865, the Great Army of the Danes landed in East Anglia; it was led by the Viking chieftains Ivar the Boneless and Halfdan, both sons of the famous Ragnar Lothbrok. Over the next fifteen years, this army methodically pushed across England, taking violent possession of area after area. They held virtual possession of Northumbria,

Mercia, and East Anglia by 871, when Alfred became king of Wessex in the middle of a sustained Danish attack against his kingdom.

Alfred bought peace from the Danes and thereby gained five years respite from their attacks, during which he struggled to amass the force necessary to repel them. In 875, when they returned to attack Wessex again, Alfred was able to fend them off; but they returned again in 878. Alfred was forced to fall back to a small fortification at Athelney in the midst of the marshes southwest of Selwood. From this base, he conducted raids against the invaders, and finally engaged the enemy at Edington and defeated him. Alfred proceeded to fortify southern England, and he advanced in 886 to London and occupied it.

The occupation of London was decisive; it was followed by a treaty between Alfred and the Danish king Guthrum, by which England was divided between them. Alfred kept control of London and southern England; Guthrum was given possession of the Danelaw, the area north of a line running roughly northwest from London to Chester. Wessex remained English, and Alfred was able to devote the last years of his life to the restoration of English learning and culture, which had been virtually destroyed by the Danes.

When Alfred died in 899, he was succeeded in turn by his son, Edward the Elder, and by his grandsons Athelstan, Edmund, and Eadred, whose reigns stretched from 899 to 955. The controlling purpose that ran through their reigns was the recovery of the Danelaw. In 910, Edward defeated a large Danish force in Staffordshire; by 924, the year of his death, he held all England south of the Humber, the traditional boundary of the southern English. His successor, Athelstan, pushed the line ever farther north and engaged combined Scandinavian, British, and Scottish forces in a battle in 937 at Brunanburh (exact location now unknown), where he won a victory celebrated in heroic verse reminiscent in style of the old epics.

Brunanburh did not mark the end of English struggles with the Danes; but to Athelstan's contemporaries, as to posterity, it seemed to mark a pivotal point in history. The England that the Danes' Great Army had invaded in 867 had been an island fragmented into separate kingdoms, with political dominance passing among them according to the chances of war and politics. The England that emerged from Brunanburh was a nation, forged in the fire of the Danish wars and united under the crown of Alfred's Wessex.

The Danes would return and the throne would be contested, but England would never return to the old political order. Brunanburh symbolized this significant transformation; the unification of England became complete in 954, during the reign of King Eadred, when Eric Bloodaxe, last of the Scandinavian kings of York, was expelled from his throne and all Northumbria was once more in English hands.

England in 955 was a country of perhaps a million people who lived in a few fair-sized towns and many small villages. London was even then the largest of the towns; estimates of its tenth-century population, and of Winchester's, vary greatly because neither city was included in the eleventh-century Domesday Survey, our main source of such statistics. But York, which was about the size of Winchester and considerably smaller than London, numbered about eight thousand inhabitants in the tenth century. Norwich and Lincoln had about five thousand inhabitants each, and a few other sizable towns—Thetford, Oxford, Colchester, Cambridge, and Ipswich—had populations between a thousand and four thousand.

Between the towns, much of the countryside was wild and desolate. Three great forest areas, the Weald, the Essex-Chiltern belt, and the Bruneswald, covered about half of the southern part of the island. Farther north, the country was less heavily wooded, though sizable forests were found here and there, notably a chain of forest lands between the Trent and Severn rivers in the western midlands. Massive stretches of marshland also isolated the separate parts of England. A large fen region covered much of East Anglia, and another, the Humber fen, formed a boundary between the northern and southern kingdoms. Despite these obstacles, travel and communication were made somewhat easier by a basic network of roads that crisscrossed the island, survivals from Roman times. Other reminders of Roman days remained here and there: abandoned towns, deserted fortresses, temples, and bridges on which the Old English tended to look with awe as "the work of giants."[2]

The center of administration of the government was London; the treasury was at Winchester. In these two cities, and on several royal estates, the king presided over a court known for its splendor and cosmopolitan character. Even in pagan days, the kings of England had surrounded themselves with wealth and material splendor; the recently excavated ship tomb of a seventh-century East Anglian king at Sutton Hoo, Suffolk, contained objects of great richness and beauty.[3] In the mid-tenth century, the greater sway of the king of all the English encouraged yet greater pomp and display: magnificent buildings, gold-inwrought tapestries, cups and other ornaments in precious metals, treasures from abroad. This age was one in which the king came to be regarded not merely as a leader of men but as God's particular agent. The king was elected by the royal council or *witan;* but, once consecrated to the throne, the king ruled not merely by the sanction of man but "by the grace of God." The elaborate coronation of King Edgar at Bath in 973, presided over by Archbishop Dunstan, is a key event in the development of the idea of English kingship: it demonstrates, in its ceremoniousness, its dignity, and its pomp, the degree to which the sanctity of the king was shown outwardly in material splendor.[4]

The political stability achieved in England by mid-century made possible the second and last period of high cultural achievement in Anglo-Saxon history. The first such period had been the late seventh and eighth centuries, when the separate kingdoms had reached an approximate balance of power and men could turn from war to art and learning. This period had been dominated culturally by Northumbria and its great figures had been Bede and Alcuin of York. Now, in the second half of the tenth century, a similar respite from political turmoil brought about a second period of cultural development, one centered, however, in the south and east midlands. Its leaders were the Benedictine monastic reformers Dunstan, Æthelwold, and Oswald; and its chief literary figure was Ælfric.

The throne of England was occupied during this half-century by Eadwig (955–959), Edgar (959–975), Edward (975–978), and Æthelred (978–1016). The events of their reigns formed a dramatic reversal, a succession of prosperity by disaster that suggests tragedy. This tragic sequence left a deep mark upon those who lived through it; its lessons formed a major theme of Ælfric and his fellow homilist Wulfstan at the end of the century.

The climax of Edgar's reign, during which art and learning flourished in an England at peace, was his coronation. Edgar was crowned when he had already reigned for fourteen years. (The coronation was perhaps delayed so long in order to hold it when Edgar reached the age of thirty, the minimum age for ordination to the priesthood.) A kind of tragic irony marked the course of the English throne in the years immediately following the coronation. Edgar died two years later, in 975; and his successor, his son Edward, was brutally murdered in the third year of his reign. The long reign of his successor Æthelred was so marked by disaster and incompetent leadership in meeting it that Æthelred was forever known by an epithet which is a bitter pun: *Æthelræd Unræd.* (*Æthelræd* meant "noble counsel"; *unræd* meant "no counsel.")

The Danes returned soon after the ten-year-old Æthelred took the throne; and, as a hundred years before, their raids rapidly grew in frequency and ferocity. But Æthelred was no Alfred, and he was surrounded by men of wavering allegiance at best. The nation's leaders adopted the fatal policy of trying to buy off the Danes and so levied a "Danegeld": a tax to raise tribute money. Six times in Æthelred's reign the tribute was paid, growing gradually heavier, as blackmail payments do. The tax drained the country; and, as the Danes grew more demanding, England grew poorer, weaker, and less able to defend herself.

Against the intricate tapestry of blackmail, deceit, and treachery that forms the political history of late tenth-century England, one episode stands out that temporarily reminded the demoralized people of their heroic past. In 991, a small English force commanded by Ealdorman Brihtnoth met a larger Viking force at Maldon. Conducting themselves by the same code that Beowulf followed, they gave the enemy the advantage and then engaged him with epic determination. A contemporary poet wove an old-fashioned heroic poem out of the result: the entire force, refusing to leave the field alive, fell beside its leader.[5]

But weakness of national leadership in England and the legendary fighting powers of the trained and disciplined Vikings from Jomsborg determined the issue. The Danish commander Swein Forkbeard launched an all-out attack against England in 1013; Æthelred fled to Normandy. This time a dramatic reversal like the one Alfred had brought about never came. After a period of additional chaos, the Dane Cnut became king of England in 1016. Danish kings held the throne until 1042, when Edward the Confessor restored the old line of Wessex. His successor, Harold, was to be the last Anglo-Saxon king; on September 28, 1066, William of Normandy disembarked with a Norman army on the shores of England.

II *The Benedictine Revival*

Against the grim chronicle of tenth-century political events must be set the story of the religious and intellectual life of Ælfric's day. For, though Ælfric's work was marked by the disasters of politics and war, the work was made possible by a general revival of cultural pursuits that flourished through the darkest hours of the close of the century. This revival was nurtured by the English monasteries under the leadership of three remarkable men: Dunstan, Æthelwold, and Oswald.[6]

Monasticism had always played an important role in English Christianity. The Celtic church had been organized around its monasteries, within each of which might be several bishops, who had no fixed dioceses, but who traveled about freely, preaching and ministering to the people. The Synod of Whitby, in 663, had spelled the end of the Celtic practice, replacing it with the diocesan organization of the Roman church. But, within the diocesan framework, monasteries continued to flourish. St. Augustine himself had founded the monastery of St. Peter and St. Paul at Canterbury; in the two hundred years after his arrival in 597, fifty or so monasteries were founded around England, if we count only those whose names survive.

The monasteries had played a dominant role in the eighth-century cultural flowering in the north. The earliest of these northern monasteries was Lindisfarne, founded by Aidan, the first missionary to Northumbria, on the island of Lindisfarne, just off the coast of Northumbria. Other early northern monasteries were at Gilling, Melrose, Tynemouth, Gateshead, and Lastingham. There were "double monasteries," with communities of both priests and nuns, at Hartlepool, Whitby, and Coldingham. Other notable monasteries were the twin houses of St. Peter at Monkwearmouth and St. Paul at Jarrow, founded in 674 and 681, respectively, by the learned Benedict Biscop. Jarrow holds a special place in the history of early English monasticism because it was the monastery where Bede spent his life.

The Danish invasions put an end to this first period of monastic glory. Lindisfarne, on its exposed, unprotected island, had borne the brunt of one of the first Danish attacks in 793. The raiders had sacked the monastery and forced the monks to take to the road, carrying the relics of their saint, Cuthbert, for a long period of wandering; and Bede's Jarrow was sacked the following year. As the Danes swept across the country, monastery after monastery fell, libraries were burned, and monks were slaughtered. When Alfred came to the throne, little was left of the monastic movement. The extent of the ruin is indicated by Alfred's famous remarks about the situation when he became king in the preface to his English translation of Gregory's *Pastoral Care:*

Swiðe feawa wæron behionan Humbre ðe hiora ðeninga cuðen understondan on Englisc, oððe furðum an ærendgewrit of Lædene on Englisc areccean; and ic wene ðæt noht monige begiondan Humbre næren. Swæ feawa hiora wæron ðæt ic furðum anne anlepne ne mæg geðencean besuðan Temese ða ða ic to rice feng .... Ða ic þa ðis eall gemunde ða gemunde ic eac hu ic geseah, ærþæmþe hit eall forheregod wære and forbærned, hu þa cirican geond eall Angelkynn stodon maðma and boca gefylda.

(There were very few on this side of the Humber who could understand their service-books in English, or even translate a letter from Latin into English; and I believe that there were not many beyond the Humber. So few there were that I cannot remember a single one south of the Thames when I came to the throne.... When I remembered all this, I remembered also how I had seen, before it had all been ravaged and burned, the churches around all England standing filled with treasures and books.)[7]

Alfred, of course, labored to restore the church and the educational system. He gathered scholars around him: Werferth, Bishop of Worcester; Plegmund, Archbishop of Canterbury; Asser, Alfred's earliest biographer. He encouraged the study of Latin; and, for those unable to read Latin, he translated or had translated a small library of indispensable books: Gregory's *Pastoral Care* and *Dialogues,* Orosius's *Universal History,* Bede's *History,* Boethius's *Consolation of Philosophy,* and part of St. Augustine's *Soliloquies.* In the marshes of Athelney, in the place from which he had organized his counterattack on the Danes, he built a new monastery, as a sign of thanksgiving. At Shaftesbury, he built a nunnery, and his daughter Æthelgifu became its abbess.

But these efforts bore little fruit in Alfred's lifetime or in the lifetimes of his immediate successors on the throne, his son Edward and his grandsons Athelstan, Edmund, and Eadred. Edward completed the New Minster his father had planned for Winchester, and he laid Alfred's body there. Alfred's widow founded a nunnery, also at Winchester. The real restoration of the monasteries, however, was to be the work of the reign of King Edgar. The leaders in this work were the three great monastic bishops: Dunstan, Bishop of Worcester and Archbishop of Canterbury; Æthelwold of Winchester; and Oswald, Archbishop of York and Dunstan's successor as Bishop of Worcester. The characters of these three men were very different;

yet they were united in the common goal of restoring English monasticism to the high place it had once held in the life of the country.

Dunstan, who was born about 909 in Somerset,[8] was of a family of high rank and was distantly related to King Edward. Dunstan spent his childhood at Glastonbury, the most ancient monastery in England, connected by tradition to Joseph of Arimathea and to King Arthur. Here he was educated and eventually became one of the brethren, though he did not yet enter into genuine monastic life. In 923, Dunstan's uncle, Athelm, became Archbishop of Canterbury; and Dunstan visited him at Canterbury and came to know the court, including the young king, Athelstan. After 926, when Athelm died, Dunstan was regularly in attendance at court, where he eventually had trouble because of the envy and distrust of some of his companions. The young Dunstan was brilliant and learned and had a wide range of interests. He was skilled in music and art and was particularly interested, it seems, in secular poetry and in the songs and legends of his people. But a strong thread of otherworldliness and mysticism ran through his character, and perhaps he was rather tactless. At any rate, it came to be rumored that he studied heathen magic and spells; after a time, when the gossip had reached the king, Dunstan was dismissed from court. Some of his enemies followed him, fell upon him, beat him, and left him in a muddy bog. Dunstan went to the house of a second episcopal uncle, Ælfheah of Winchester. Here, at the age of twenty-six, as he recovered from his experience at court and as he talked with his uncle, he began to acquire the sense of a great mission for his life: the restoration of English monasticism.

The decline of English monasticism in the ninth century had not been an isolated phenomenon; it had been matched by a parallel decline on the Continent. But, in 935, a strong reform movement had been working for twenty-five years to restore the monasteries. The form which this movement took was a return to the observance of the Benedictine Rule, the directions laid down by the founder of the order for the regulation of monastic life, or the development of these directions in the ninth century by Benedict of Aniane. The *Capitulare Monasticum* of Benedict of Aniane required uniformity in all monasteries concerning the daily schedule of prayers, the rules of conduct, even the amounts of food served. Monks were to keep silence, to avoid any but the most necessary contacts with the world, to observe the strictest obedience to spiritual guardians, and to follow a rigorous daily routine of worship and prayer.

Opposed to this demanding way of life was the tradition formulated by the eighth-century St. Chrodegang of Metz, by which monasteries could be formed of clergymen who lived together under rule but who were unbound by the Benedictine vows and who could own property and even live apart from the monastery. These permissive practices had spread widely, not only in France but also in England.

The beginning of reform on the Continent had been the establishment of a monastery at Cluny in Burgundy in 910. From this center, the reform movement spread to other monasteries: notably Fleury on the Loire and Ghent and St. Omer in Flanders. It is uncertain how much influence these Continental reforms had upon the young Dunstan; but, under the guidance of Ælfheah of Winchester, he began to formulate ambitions for similar reforms in England. The prospect of renouncing secular life was at first daunting to him; but, after a critical illness, he decided to become a monk and to labor to restore regular monasticism in England. This decision was taken about 936. He took up residence at Glastonbury and began to gather around him other monks who would follow the Benedictine Rule.

King Athelstan died in 939 and was succeeded by his brother Edmund, a great friend of Dunstan. The new king immediately revoked Dunstan's banishment and recalled him to court. But again the old gossip of dark learning was circulated and Edmund banished Dunstan, as his brother had done before him. This time, however, something happened in which Dunstan's early biographers were to see the hand of God. Edmund, on a hunting trip, in a wild chase after a stag, narrowly escaped being carried to his death over a precipice. In the moments before his horse jerked to a stop, he thought of Dunstan and of the injustice he himself had done him. Returning from the hunt, he summoned Dunstan, took him to Glastonbury, and installed him there as abbot; Dunstan was at last in a position to put into practice his plans for the revival of the monasteries.

In the forty-five years that remained of his life, Dunstan labored to carry out his purpose, first as abbot of Glastonbury for thirteen years; then—after a year of exile as the result of personal friction with King Eadwig and his advisers—as Bishop of Worcester and London for three years; and finally as Archbishop of Canterbury for twenty-eight years.

The second key figure in the monastic movement was Æthelwold, Bishop of Winchester from 963 until 984.[9] Æthelwold, who was born in Winchester, came under the influence of Ælfheah at about the same time Dunstan did; as a matter of fact, they were consecrated to the priesthood by Ælfheah on the same day. Æthelwold entered the cloister at Glastonbury while Dunstan was abbot there and learned the Benedictine life. In 954, he requested permission to go abroad to study Benedictine practices more thoroughly; in order to persuade him to stay in England, King Eadred made him abbot of a small and poor monastery at Abingdon. Here he plunged into the labor of restoring the ruined buildings, of building a new church, and of instituting strict obedience to the Rule of St. Benedict. In the years that followed, Æthelwold, as abbot of Abingdon, and after 963, as Bishop of Winchester, strove to extend even farther the work of Dunstan.

Archbishop Oswald, the third of the leaders of the reform, received, as Dunstan and Æthelwold had, the initial impulse toward his mission at Winchester, though by the time Oswald arrived there Ælfheah was dead and Æthelwold had not yet arrived to install regular monks in place of the secular clerks who led an easy life there.[10] Growing dissatisfied with his life at Winchester, Oswald left England and went to Fleury, where he enthusiastically embraced the study of the Rule. In 961, soon after his return to England, he became Dunstan's successor as Bishop of Worcester and continued his work of restoration and reform.

The prominence of Dunstan, Æthelwold, and Oswald in the history of the tenth-century monastic reform is perhaps due to the circumstance that each was the subject of a biography written soon after his death. Undoubtedly, many others led in the movement, for it was a widespread and lasting activity. But we know something of what each of these men did, for each left the mark of a strong personality upon the history of his time. The character of Dunstan emerges clearly from the record of his deeds and from the pages of his first biography. If the repeated incidents of antagonism and envy toward him indicate a certain austerity and perhaps tactlessness in his personality, another side of his character emerges in the biographer's accounts of his dreams, visions, and prophecies. He seems to have been a man to whom the line between this world and the next was very thin, for dreams and reality were, to him, inextricably mixed. Perhaps the repeated accusations of witchcraft stem from this quality. As a reformer, Dunstan's policy was temperate; he apparently did not attempt to bring about sudden changes in practice. At Worcester and later at the abbey at Canterbury, secular clerks continued to serve. But, as opportunity arose, he filled their posts with men who would carry on the work of reform. Glastonbury was his particular care; from the monastery there, monks went out, with his encouragement, to rebuild and reinvigorate monastic life throughout southern England.

Eleanor Duckett has characterized Æthelwold as "a man full of rushing energy, impetuous, driven by a single purpose, unencumbered by scruple of policies to be weighed and balanced."[11] If Dunstan was the man of visions of the reform, Æthelwold was the man of action. His character appears clearly in the story of his reform of the Old Minster at Winchester. When Æthelwold arrived as bishop in 963, he found the choir filled with secular clerks, many married, many given to gluttony and drunkenness (according to Ælfric's account). After he had given them some time to reform their manner of living, Æthelwold's patience ended. Appearing before the door of the cathedral one Sunday morning, he ordered those who would to take the monastic vows and those who would not to leave. The furious clerks stormed out and appealed to King Edgar, who referred the matter to Dunstan, who agreed with Æthelwold; the order remained; the clerks did not return.

But Æthelwold's influence was not merely negative; he was a great builder and a patron of art and learning. From Winchester, his influence went out to restore and rebuild monastery after ruined monastery: at Milton in Dorset, at Chertsey in Surrey, and especially in the eastern fen country: Medeshamstede, Ely, and Thorney.

But, if Dunstan supplied a quiet leadership from Canterbury and Æthelwold supplied fervor and aggressiveness to the movement, Oswald brought persistence and practicality. It was he who carried forward the restoration of Worcester that Dunstan had begun. He brought scholars from France to teach the discipline to English monks, he worked out methods for the use of monastic lands that later served as models, and he worked to record and systematize his work and that of his fellow reformers. Like Æthelwold, he established many monasteries and saw that they prospered: Winchcombe, Pershore, Evesham, Crowland, and others.

If the work of the monastic reformers had been merely the alteration of monastic routine, their labors would have had little long-range impact. But their aim was higher, their achievement greater. In the environment that they created, old books could be studied again and new ones written. Art was cultivated, most notably in the work of the "Winchester School" and in the architecture of the newly rebuilt monasteries. Alongside Latin, English prose came to be valued, not only in the works of Ælfric, but also in those of Wulfstan and others. The reformers reached outside the monasteries to reform English life itself, and they succeeded in making England once again, for a while, a place where art and learning could flourish.

III *The Intellectual Temper*

Also important in reading tenth-century literature is some knowledge of the intellectual temper of the times. It is impossible to deal with this subject adequately in a few paragraphs; but, at the risk of oversimplification, we may describe briefly three clusters of ideas and values which, in various forms, pervaded and shaped Anglo-Saxon life on all levels and which were still very much alive in the tenth century. These are the pagan Germanic heritage, the Classical heritage, and the Christian heritage.

We know little about the scope of pagan ideas and traditions in Anglo-Saxon life,[12] but it must have been greater than the surviving ecclesiastical documents suggest. The Anglo-Saxons, we know, never lost their sense of kinship with their Germanic kinsmen on the Continent; as a matter of fact, this sense of kinship led to the very early and fairly extensive missionary efforts from English Christians to the Germanic tribes. And intellectual leaders in England from Bede to Dunstan, we are told, took an interest in the songs and legends of the pagan past. Even through the clerical filters, we can see pagan traditions and beliefs persisting throughout the Old English period, especially among the common people. A charm for making one's land fertile invokes Erce, mother of earth; Bede mentions a midwinter festival called the "night of the mothers"; the boar-emblems on the helmets in *Beowulf* recall that the boar was sacred to the pagan god Freyr. Place-names in England even today recall the names of Germanic gods: Woden (Woodnesborough, Wednesbury, etc.), Thunor (Thunderfield, Thurstable), and Tiw (Tysoe, Tuesley). As late as Ælfric, preachers felt the need to attack from the pulpit charms, fortune-telling, and other superstitions of a pagan coloring.[13] The pagan gods were sometimes preserved into Christian literature as devils and ogres, like the monstrous creatures in *Beowulf*. And perhaps a vestige of pagan religion lingers in the ambiguous "fate," so often referred to in Old English poetry; though it is hard to find a particular use of the term which is irreconcilable with Christianity.

Ultimately more important than these random vestiges of paganism is the persistence through the Old English period of a pattern of social relationships and ethical values derived from pagan Germanic society. This has been called the "heroic code," or the "*comitatus* ideal." This cluster of ideas, sometimes merged with analogous Christian ideas, was an important element in Anglo-Saxon life. At the center of the code was the ideal of loyalty, which found its fullest expression in heroic society in the relationship between a man and his lord. Each lord was surrounded by a band of followers: the *gesithas*, "companions." These followers were favored by the lord in time of peace with gifts and "hall-joy"; they repaid these favors in time of war by a fierce loyalty which extended to giving their lives to protect or avenge the lord. This loyalty was primarily a personal one, not a generalized "patriotism."

The chief virtue of the lord, in heroic terms, was liberality or munificence. In the heroic poems, gifts are frequently given spontaneously or as a token of gratitude for unusual service. Thus, after Beowulf vanquishes Grendel, Hrothgar ceremoniously presents him with a golden standard and a banner, armor, a famous treasure-sword, and eight horses; the grandeur of the gifts is described in lingering detail by the poet. More prosaic was the lord's gift of armor and horses to a new follower; such a gift came to be a legal obligation, known as the *heriot* and governed by specific rules. For example, the *heriot* was to be repaid to the lord on the man's death, unless he fell in battle. Such gifts were apparently felt to be symbolic of more substantial favors: gifts of land and the bestowal of personal protection.

The follower, in return, owed his lord absolute loyalty to the death. If the lord fell in battle, his survivors were to fight, no matter what the odds, until they fell beside him. Similarly, the "companions" were to be prepared to follow their lord into exile, if need be; or, if he were killed, they were to exact complete vengeance upon his killers. No action was regarded with more abhorrence than disloyalty or betrayal of a lord to whom one owed allegiance.

The bonds of loyalty between a man and his lord were paralleled by those which bound a man to his kinsmen. Throughout Germanic society, the ties of blood relationship were held very dear. To a kinsman, a man owed many obligations; it was his responsibility to arrange for the marriage of the unmarried women of his family, to set the terms of marriage agreements, and to continue to protect the wife's interests even after the marriage. He was to provide for the rearing of young orphaned kinsmen and to see that kinsmen accused of crimes not only came forward to answer the charges but also received justice at the hands of the law. The chief recorded expression of these ties, however, was the code of vengeance, by which a man exacted payment—in blood or in money—for the murder of a kinsman. The vendetta was in the nature of a sacred obligation; it transcended personal feelings and was regulated by exact conventions and agreements. If vengeance was originally a spontaneous and unregulated action, by the time of our earliest knowledge of it, it had become surrounded by carefully detailed legal conventions. Payment in money or property could be accepted in lieu of blood vengeance; in the laws of Alfred, the amounts of such payments were carefully fixed as *wergilds*.

The heroic codes of the *comitatus* and of blood vengeance find frequent expression in the older poetry. *Beowulf*, for example, may be seen as the expression of an intricate series of interlocking patterns of heroic loyalties: between Beowulf and Hrothgar and Hygelac, between Beowulf the young warrior and his "companions," between Beowulf the aged king and his people, and so on. The ancient poem *Widsith* is a roll-call of heroic names and deeds celebrating, through the voice of a fictitious wandering minstrel, the munificence of great kings and the deeds by which their followers repay them. The lament of "The Wanderer" is for the loss of the lord and the sorrow of the breaking of heroic ties.

But these codes were by no means moribund in the tenth century, neither in poetry nor in practice. The poem of *Maldon* tells how the followers of Brihtnoth fought the Danes, against hopeless odds, to fall beside their leader. The various tales of cowardice and treachery in the reign of King Æthelred were particularly abhorrent because of the general consciousness of the heroic ideal, against which such deeds stood out in horrid contrast. *Maldon* provided by no means the only example of the heroic code in action from the late tenth century, for Streonwold's men chose the same course in Devon in 988, and the men of the East Angles met a similar fate in 1004.

Old English life may be thought of, then, as set in a matrix of ancient pagan belief which found expression in persistent superstition and perhaps even worship and in the pervasive influence of traditional codes of behavior. Christianity, inevitably, modified the pagan traditions; but it seldom succeeded in erasing them. For the most part, it did not even attempt to do so. Paganism and Christianity came to stand in a complex relationship in Anglo-Saxon England, an interweaving so intricate that the fabric cannot be separated.[14]

Just as Pope Gregory suggested that Christian churches be built on sites where pagans were accustomed to worship, so the church for the most part transmuted and accommodated the heroic structure of social relationships and beliefs rather than attempting to eradicate it. The loyalty which man owes to God is often referred to in terms of the old heroic code, but this loyalty does not replace man's loyalty owed also to earthly lords. The church added its spiritual power to the oaths of allegiance, and even condoned deeds of violence undertaken in defense of a lord or in vengeance for him. Alcuin, in 801, praises, for example, a man who had "boldly avenged his lord"; and Ælfric's contemporary, Archbishop Wulfstan, in 1014 condemns betraying a lord's soul as being even worse than betraying one's military oaths to him.

Christian teaching is everywhere fitted into the heroic frame of reference. Christ is the great lord; the disciples, his thanes. The sin of Judas, then, takes on the loathsome coloring of heroic disloyalty. Man is bound to God by the ties of the heroic code; God dispenses favors like a Germanic lord and demands in return faithful service. Heaven is like the hall of the lord; the bliss of the saints, the "hall-joy" of heroes. All men are brothers and are bound by ties like those which bind blood-kinsmen.

The code of vengeance was harder to reconcile with Christianity than the code of loyalty. The church seems to have encouraged settlements of feuds by payment of *wergilds* rather than by bloodshed and to have invoked heavy penances on those who resolved feuds by violence. At the same time, it was careful to establish *wergilds* for its own members; these *wergilds* were to be paid to the monasteries and were enforced by royal power. Moreover, even the social structure of the Old English church seems to have owed something to the heroic patterns, in its groupings of priests and monks around bishops and abbots, from whom they received protection and to whom they owed loyalty.

All these interpenetrations of paganism and Christianity resulted in a Christianity in England of a peculiarly native coloring which gained strength from its roots in racial and tribal traditions. These roots also ran back, of course, to Celtic culture, the inheritance of the church from its British and Irish sides. The victory at the Synod of Whitby in 663 for Roman usages did not end the influence upon the church of Irish Christianity, with its unrestrained and often exotic mysticism; its tendencies toward extreme asceticism; its emphasis upon simplicity, poverty, and humility. It is hard to gauge the continuing influence of this aspect of the church, but it is often recognizable in the legends of saints and in the vision literature of the period.[15]

The view that Western culture is a product of the fusion of Germanic and Roman cultures has been thoroughly developed by Christopher Dawson.[16] Rome did not contribute only Roman Christianity to Northern culture of the Dark Ages; it also transmitted to England, as to all of Northern Europe, the heritage of secular Classical culture. Historians of the last fifty years have uncovered more and more evidence of cultural ties between England and the Mediterranean world, ties reaching back to the Stone and Bronze Ages. Evidence of very early ties with the Aegean world and the East is to be found in the art forms and techniques of both the British and the Anglo-Saxons. The designs of the treasures from Sutton Hoo, for instance, have been linked not only with Sweden, but also with Byzantium and the eastern Mediterranean. Traffic with the Mediterranean world seems to have been heavy and steady throughout the Anglo-Saxon period. The older view of an island completely de-Romanized by the time of the Augustinian mission in 597 has been largely replaced by a belief that Roman influence must have been still fairly strong in England in the sixth century. This influence was renewed by a new wave of missionaries late in the seventh century: Theodore, Hadrian, and others, who quickly brought Classical learning to such a point in England that Aldhelm could boast that England surpassed Ireland in learning. In this environment appeared Bede, who has been called "one of the greatest 'classic' minds of the Middle Ages." Even the author of *Beowulf* may have been indebted to Virgil's *Aeneid*.

The most eloquent description of the characteristic Anglo-Saxon fusion of Northern heroic, barbarian culture, and Roman

Christianity and Classicism has been made by Clinton Albertson. His summary deserves quotation: "The Anglo-Saxons' literature is then, like their culture, an amalgam, but a rich, vibrant, fascinating amalgam, like the pages of the Lindisfarne Gospels. It is the autobiography of the heroic northern mind becoming Roman and western. It is not the case of an old northern tradition revised by western monks . . . . The best of Anglo-Saxon literature is a new *creation*, a oneness resultant upon this cultural fusion, not just the jointed work of later pious revisers."[17]

As we shall see, Ælfric's homilies, in their way, express this oneness brought out of multiplicity, as *Beowulf* does in its way. His constant interpretation of biblical and Christian material in terms of local culture, his moral fervor, his love of clarity and common sense, his eminent practicality—all reflect the mingled intellectual traditions of his England.

IV *Ælfric's Birth and Childhood*

Only the broad outlines of Ælfric's life are visible to us after the passage of a millennium. We know about when he was born, about when he died, and a few general things about the way he spent his life and the order in which he composed the works for which we remember him. And even these few bits of information are the result of fairly recent scholarly inquiry; for centuries, the very identity of Ælfric was unknown, even while his works were the subject of antiquarian and scholarly dispute. It should be remembered, however, that Ælfric's biography, scanty as it is, is more complete than that of many a more prominent man of the centuries before the modern practice of keeping voluminous records began. For Cynewulf, we have only a name; and we lack even that for the *Beowulf* poet. We know at least enough of Ælfric's life to establish a loose chronology of his works and the key events of his life.[18]

Ælfric seems to have been born about the middle of the 950s, perhaps in 955. We know that he was sent to the monastery of Cernel in 987 and that he was a priest at the time. If we assume ordination at the customary age of thirty and a lapse of about two years before his departure for Cernel, we can date his ordination in 985 and his birth in 955. It is fairly certain that he was a native of Wessex, for the consistently West-Saxon forms of his language betray no trace of another origin.

The circumstances of his life indicate that his family was of the middle class. He remained a simple priest until the age of fifty, when he became an abbot. His advancement would probably have been more rapid if he had been of aristocratic birth, for the Anglo-Saxon church liked to place men in positions of authority who could deal with their secular counterparts on a fairly equal social basis. For the same reason, it is unlikely that he was from a family of the lower class; for, if he had been, he probably would never have become an abbot. His tone of address to men of power and position (to Ealdorman Æthelmær, for example) has the modest confidence of one who respects but is unawed by high rank. Such confidence might come, of course, from a sense of his intellectual and ecclesiastical dignity alone, but the impression given is otherwise.

Like most medieval writers, Ælfric tells us nothing of himself personally except occasionally to illustrate some objective point. The only comment he makes on his early life appears in the preface to Genesis, in which, to illustrate the low state of Latin learning prevailing in England, he cites the priest with whom he began the study of Latin. The man could understand "a little Latin," Ælfric says, but he did not understand even the difference between the Old Law of the Old Testament and the New Law (Crawford, 76).

A middle-class boyhood in Wessex in the mid-tenth century, with some beginning instruction in Latin: beyond this general idea of Ælfric's early life, we can only move into the realm of speculation. Marguerite-Marie Dubois points out that the Latin tutor, the Wessex setting, and the probably upper-middle-class status suggest certain kinds of positions for Ælfric's father.[19] He might have been a member of the king's personal retinue, what Bede called the *comites* and Alfred called the *gesith*. Or he might have been a merchant. Dubois also points out that Ælfric is almost certain to have had brothers, since it was not the practice of Anglo-Saxon parents to end the family line by consecrating only sons to the church. But such castings of probability, reasonable as they may be, are unverifiable and lead nowhere.

V *Ælfric at Winchester*

Whatever the circumstances of Ælfric's early life, sometime in the early 970s he entered the monastic school at Winchester. The date is unknown; Ælfric says in his *Letter to the Monks of Eynsham* that he lived in Æthelwold's school "many years." Since Æthelwold died in 984, Ælfric may have been at Winchester by 970 or shortly thereafter.

Æthelwold had come to Winchester as bishop from his notable successes at Abingdon in 963. After his sensational expulsion of the secular clergy, he had set forth upon a characteristically vigorous program of reform. Æthelgar, one of his disciples, was established as abbot of the monastery, and here, as well as in the nunnery, the Benedictine discipline was quickly established. Æthelwold himself planned and oversaw the building of a magnificent new church, which was completed and dedicated with great ceremony in 971. The consecration was attended by King Edgar and Archbishop Dunstan; the high point of the proceedings was the removal of the bones of St. Swithun from their grave outside the church to a new tomb by the high altar of the new church. (Swithun had been Bishop of Winchester in the mid-ninth century.) The disinterment of his relics had been accompanied by miraculous events and healings, many of which Ælfric later described in his saint's life of Swithun (*LS* XXI).

By the time Ælfric entered the monastic school there, Winchester had become the intellectual center of the reform movement. Æthelwold himself, though he had many other obligations at court and in the other monasteries whose progress he supervised, apparently took an active role in the work of the school. In his Latin life of the bishop, Ælfric says that Æthelwold took particular pleasure in teaching personally the students at Winchester and in "exhorting them with pleasant words to better things" (*V. Æ.,* 223). The scriptorium had been founded by Swithun himself; now, under Æthelwold's leadership, it was reinvigorated and craftsmen gathered here to produce a series of notable examples of the bookmaker's art. Shortly before Ælfric's arrival, Godemann, one of the most accomplished of the Winchester artists, had produced the Benedictional which still survives, bearing Æthelwold's name. Here, too, somewhat later, was produced the Tropary of Æthelred, compiled for use with the new organ of the cathedral.[20]

For the monks, life under the Rule at Winchester was firmly oriented around the liturgy, around the service of God by prayer and ceremony.[21] The exact schedule followed by the medieval monastery is hard to reconstruct, for the surviving *horaria* or timetables do not indicate "clock time" but merely the sequence of exercises.[22] Also, there were three timetables according to the season: winter, summer, and Lent. Here is an example of a typical monastic day, based on the Regularis Concordia for the winter season:

2:00 A.M.	Monks go to choir for prayer and psalms, followed by Lauds (or Matins) and Lauds of All Saints and of the dead.
Dawn	Prime, followed by psalms and prayers.
6:45	Reading in the cloister; private masses for those who were priests.
8:00	Monks return to the dormitory to wash and dress, then go back to the church for Terce and the "morning Mass."
9:00	Chapter, which might include a spiritual conference and the confession of faults.
9:45–12:30	Work.
12:30	Sext, followed by the sung High Mass and None.
2:00	Dinner (the only meal of the day).
3:00	Reading.
5:00	Vespers, Matins of the dead. A drink was served in the refectory, followed by a short public reading in choir, and Compline.
7:00	Monks retire for the night.

These times are all approximate, for the monks lived by "sun time"; and their day lengthened and shortened according to the season. During the summer, there was a second period of sleep between the night office and Prime, and two meals were served rather than one, the second about 6 P.M. Such was the daily routine followed by Ælfric from early youth through the rest of his life.

The monastic school at Winchester was basically a school for the training of monks.[23] Child oblation—the dedication of a young child to the monastic life—was common, and it was necessary to train these children in reading, the recitation of the offices, singing, and the other necessary monastic skills. In addition, despite occasional opposition, most monastic schools like Winchester accepted as pupils local children not destined for the monastic life, especially the sons of the nobility.

The curriculum was based upon the *trivium* (grammar, rhetoric, and dialectic) and the *quadrivium* (arithmetic, geometry, music, and astronomy), though in a weakened form, oriented for the most part toward the practical needs of monastic life. The first and most basic study was grammar, which meant the study of the Latin language and its literature. The first four years or so of a student's career was devoted to learning to read and write Latin, with some attention perhaps to metrics and the elements of rhetoric. This groundwork was followed by reading in Latin literature of the church, especially lives of saints, patristic biblical commentaries, and ecclesiastical history. Of the *quadrivium*, the subjects stressed were arithmetic and astronomy (or cosmography), especially in their application to the calendar and the computation of feast-days. Music, of course, was the study of plain-song, for use in the services.

Ælfric's education, of course, went far beyond the basic curriculum. The extent of his literary study is clear from the sources of his works, particularly his homilies; he was probably the best-educated man in the England of his day. But, as a monastic student and later as a teacher, his work was oriented toward the simple outlines of the monastic curriculum.

After about ten years of study, Ælfric, as a candidate for the priesthood, would have embarked on studies more specifically directed toward ordination, further study of theology and study of priestly duties. If he followed the typical pattern, he would have taken minor orders in adolescence, become a deacon at about twenty-five, and been ordained a priest at the canonical age of thirty.

VI *Ælfric at Cernel*

The first date in Ælfric's life which can be established with any certainty is 987, when he left the monastery at Winchester to go to a new monastery at Cernel (now Cerne Abbas), in Dorset. The foundation charter of this abbey is still preserved.[24] It was begun during King Edgar's reign, when so much development in monasticism took place; it was to be a memorial to the hermit Eadwold, the pious brother of King Edmund of East Anglia, who had been martyred by the Danes in 870. Eadwold's hermitage was thought to have been near the spot where the new monastery was to stand.

The founder of the new monastery was Æthelmær, a prominent nobleman who came to have great influence over the course of

Ælfric's later life. Æthelmær's father was Æthelweard, ealdorman of the province which included present-day Devon, Somerset, and Dorset. The office of ealdorman was a high one; he was the king's representative in the area; and, in a country as yet only loosely unified, he had power which sometimes rivaled that of the king himself. Æthelweard, a powerful patron of learning and the monastic movement, was something of a scholar himself: he contributed to the Anglo-Saxon Chronicle and wrote a Latin chronicle of his own, based upon Bede, Isidore, and the Anglo-Saxon Chronicle.[25] He was also apparently the patron of the restoration of Pershore Abbey in Worcestershire during Edgar's reign. Æthelweard died around the turn of the century, perhaps in 1002; until his death, he and his son Æthelmær were a continual influence on Ælfric, suggesting scholarly work for him and encouraging him in it.

It seems probable that Ælfric was sent to Cernel in order to teach the new monks there the Benedictine Rule and to organize the teaching program there. It was the custom to extend the reform into new monasteries in this way; Oswald brought the scholarly monk Abbo to Ramsey from Fleury, a center of the Continental reform, for a similar purpose. Ælfric was to remain at Cernel as a scholar-teacher for eighteen years. When he left, in 1005, it was to become abbot of yet another new monastery, also founded by Æthelmær, at Eynsham. The main body of Ælfric's writing was done at Cernel, and it grew directly out of his teaching young boys in the monastic school, older monks the Rule and more advanced studies, and laymen in the parish church on Æthelmær's estates.

Recent students of Ælfric's work have come to see that it reflects a consistent and long-range plan.[26] In the preface to his first collection of homilies, he suggests something of the origins of this plan. It occurred to him, he says, to translate this material from Latin into English because he had seen and heard many errors in the existing English books, which might lead unlearned men astray (*CH* I, p. 2). At Cernel, we may believe, as elsewhere in England, there was great need for learning in both English and Latin. Knowledge of Latin had declined until many priests themselves could not read the material they needed. This situation needed to be remedied; but, in the interim, it was essential that fundamental material be made available in clear, accurate, English translation.

Therefore, Ælfric embarked on a program of composition, adaptation, and translation on a very large scale; but the work was conjoined by a few simple aims. First, he set about presenting in a clear form the basic teachings of the church in such a way that laymen could understand them. Second, he presented in a similarly clear form other material useful to priests and monks in carrying out their work. And third, he produced material to be used in the teaching of Latin soundly and effectively to the students of the monastic school, so the next generation of clerics would not have to rely on English translations.

The doctrine that Ælfric presented amounted to a survey of universal history. He set forth the central facts of the Old Testament and of the "Old Law," the facts of Christ's Incarnation and the "New Law," and the essential stages in the spread of Christianity throughout the world, first by the apostles and then by the martyrs and confessors. The conclusion of this Augustinian world historical view was the Day of Judgment. Other works amplified this plan by giving accounts of the physical world, instructing parish priests in their duties, and teaching monks how to live in the monastic way.

Ælfric's plan inevitably suggests comparison with King Alfred's, of the previous century. Like Ælfric's, Alfred's plan was intended to counter the widespread decline in learning of his day, the aftermath of the Danish depredations. Alfred aimed, like Ælfric, at providing in English, for those ignorant of Latin, texts which set forth knowledge basic to faith. His works, too, fit into a consistent, overall plan which includes material about the physical world (Orosius's *History*), about the rise of Christianity in England (Bede's *History*), and about basic moral and philosophical teachings (Gregory's *Pastoral Care,* Boethius's *Consolation of Philosophy,* and Augustine's *Soliloquies*). Ælfric knew Alfred's work, of course, and no doubt drew general inspiration from it. But his plan differs from Alfred's in being of far greater scope and in being designed directly for particular groups: monastic students, monks and priests, and laymen.

It is possible that Ælfric had conceived his plan and had begun to carry it out even before he left Winchester, for he appears to have completed his first volume of homilies in 989, only two years after he went to Cernel. This volume, the first series of *Catholic Homilies,* consists of forty homilies arranged according to the church year. A second series, completed in 992, adds forty more homilies arranged according to the same plan. Ælfric suggests, in the Latin preface to the first series, that the two volumes be kept separate, one being read in church one year, the other the next. But he gives his permission for homilies from the two series to be combined, if anyone wishes to do so (*CH* II, p. 2). Taken together, the eighty homilies of the two volumes of *Catholic Homilies* constitute a fairly comprehensive survey of Christian world history, from Creation to the final Judgment. The first piece in the double series, "On the Beginning of Creation" (*CH* I. I), is not assigned to a particular day but is to be preached "when you wish"; and it stands as a kind of general introduction to the two volumes. It gives an account of the events in Genesis, the life of Christ, and the Last Judgment, thus presenting, in brief form, the essentials of both the Old Law and the New.

Ælfric next turned, it seems (though it is impossible to be sure of exact chronology), to a subject which was a basic part of the medieval curriculum: cosmography. The practical application of the study of astronomy and the solar year was the calculation of church festivals and especially Easter. The computation of Easter was a matter of controversy for centuries; it was, among other things, the chief specific point of difference between the Celtic church and the Roman one. Ælfric's modest treatise on the subject, *De Temporibus Anni,* treats the divisions of time and of the solar year, the basic principles of astronomy, and the phenomenon of the atmosphere. Ælfric's sources are Bede's astronomical works, but he adapts them very freely and adds some material not found in Bede.

About 995, Ælfric produced another group of works with a clear relevance to his general plan: his *Grammar,* a Latin-English *Glossary,* and a textbook in the form of a Latin dialogue, the *Colloquy.* Ælfric's sense of the close relation between the *Grammar* and his other translations is clear from his preface, in which he says he decided to translate Priscian's Latin grammar after he had translated the two volumes of homilies, because grammar is "seo cæg, ðe ðæra boca andgit unlic" (the key which unlocks the meaning of those books) (Zupitza, 2). Ælfric's *Glossary* is appended to about half of the fifteen manuscripts of the *Grammar.* The items are arranged according to subject, beginning with words having to do with God and Creation, continuing with the names of "members"—of the body, of society, and of the family—and ending with lists of birds, fish, animals, etc. The little Latin dialogue, the *Colloquy,* has attracted wide interest not only because it is one of the only pieces in a semidramatic form from the Old English period but because of its rare series of miniatures describing the daily lives of common people. A master asks questions of students, who assume the roles of representatives of various occupations. The result is a vivid, though brief, panorama of Anglo-Saxon life.

Ælfric's next book was a major work, which, like the *Catholic Homilies* and the Latin instructional material, requires closer examination later. This work was the *Lives of Saints*, another collection of forty pieces. This compilation, according to the English preface which heads it, was made at the specific request of Æthelweard and Æthelmær, but it obviously fits closely into Ælfric's larger purposes. In the same preface, Ælfric distinguishes sharply between this volume and the two volumes of homilies which preceded it. The saints' lives in the volumes of homilies celebrate saints whose feast-days are honored by the laity. These new lives deal with saints whose days are celebrated only by the monks (*LS* p. 4). Furthermore, these new pieces are for the most part not homilies, written to be read aloud in church, but are designed to be read privately, though in form they are similar and obviously might furnish material for homilies. Thirty-one of the pieces are of this kind; six others are homilies (*LS* I, XII, XIII, and XVI–XVIII), and three items at the end seem separate from the rest: the *Interrogationes, De Falsis Deis,* and *De XII Abusivis.* Again, one item seems intended to serve as a general introduction to the whole series: number XVI, "The Memory of the Saints," which outlines the types of saints and speaks in general of their significance. One of the items appended to the *Lives* deserves particular notice: the *Interrogationes Sigewulfi in Genesin,* an English translation of a handbook on Genesis written by the eighth-century English scholar Alcuin in the form of catechetical questions and answers on Genesis and dedicated to his pupil Sigewulf.

Another group of works which belongs primarily to the period at Cernel is the Bible translations and adaptations. These translations give Ælfric a permanent place in the history of the Bible in English, and seem clearly to fit into his broad plan of instruction. Nevertheless, he seems to have felt considerable reluctance to undertake such work. In the Old English preface to Genesis (Crawford, 76), Ælfric addresses Æthelweard, reminding him of his requests for a translation of Genesis. The task seemed burdensome and uncongenial to him, Ælfric says; but Æthelweard had told him that he needed to translate only as far as Isaac since someone else had translated the rest. In the texts that survive, it appears that Ælfric did translate only as far as Chapter xxiv, though later editors added the rest of Genesis by the other translator and versions of Exodus, Leviticus, and Deuteronomy to his Genesis translation, a section of Numbers that he had translated, and his epitomes of Joshua and Judges to produce the so-called *Old English Heptateuch.* Ælfric, of course, had translated a number of biblical passages in the course of composing his homilies; and he had made free versions, mostly highly condensed, of the books of Kings (*LS* XVIII), the Maccabees (*LS* XXV), Esther (Assmann VIII), and Judith (Assmann IX). The homiletic paraphrase of Job (*CH* II. XXXV) is sometimes spoken of as a translation as well.

This list of Ælfric's works while at Cernel may be concluded with the *Hexameron,* the *Admonitio,* and the *Letter for Wulfsige.* The *Hexameron* is a very free treatment of St. Basil's *Hexameron*, or "account of the week of Creation." Ælfric also includes in this work material drawn from Bede's commentaries on Genesis. The *Admonitio* is an English version of St. Basil's *Admonitio ad Filium Spiritualem,* and it seems intended for the instruction of new monks. In a series of short chapters, it presents commentaries on the virtues of faithful monks, such as chastity, love of God and of one's neighbor, and the avoidance of worldliness and avarice. The *Letter for Wulfsige* was written at the request of the Bishop of Sherborne, who wanted a pastoral letter on the duties of the clergy to be sent to all clergymen in his diocese. Ælfric begins with a short personal letter to Wulfsige, and then divides the main body of the letter into two parts, the first consisting of thirty-five short sections; the second, of two longer sections. The subjects covered in the first part include the need for celibacy, the division of the orders, and the behavior of a good priest. Most of the second part is devoted to instructions about the Eucharist. An interesting detail of the work is the warning in Section xxxv against funerals because of the "heathenism which is there committed."

In addition to these and a few smaller works, Ælfric, during his time at Cernel, continued to revise and develop his homilies for the church year. Peter Clemoes has meticulously reconstructed the general outlines of these revisions and expansions.[27] Ælfric, it appears, expanded his series of homilies in two stages, which Clemoes chooses to call Temporale Homilies I and II. Temporale Homilies I, which must have consisted of about forty items (Ælfric's customary number), was a series of homilies, using many from the two series of *Catholic Homilies,* from the Proper of the Season to the Sunday after Pentecost. Temporale Homilies II must have been a two-volume series of approximately eighty homilies, which extended the series through the entire year. The second volume survives in an imperfect form (Trinity College, Cambridge, B.15.34); the first, which perhaps contained prefaces, is lost. Altogether, Clemoes lists over a hundred extant homilies of Ælfric; some others must have been lost; but Ælfric's work was circulated so much that probably most of his homilies do survive.

By the time Ælfric left Cernel in 1005, his overall plan of education was generally complete. For laymen, he had written several series of homilies which set forth clearly and gracefully the central elements of the Christian faith. He had also translated into English selections from the Bible that he believed most important in understanding the preparation under the Old Law for the New. For monks and priests he had compiled a reading book of texts which told of their outstanding predecessors in the dissemination of the faith, and he had written a simple handbook of clerical duties and responsibilities. For the boys in the monastic school, he had provided Latin texts that would lead them into an elementary knowledge sounder than that he had received from his first teacher.

VII *Ælfric at Eynsham*

In 1005, or possibly the year before, Ælfric moved to Eynsham, in present-day Oxfordshire, as abbot of a new monastery there. The foundation charter of Eynsham still survives and is of considerable interest to students of Ælfric. It is even possible that Ælfric wrote the charter himself, for it is in the clear, graceful Latin of Ælfric's other Latin works.[28] The charter indicates that the monastery was built by the Æthelmær who had built Cernel and who had been Ælfric's patron there. Æthelweard had died, probably in 1002; and Æthelmær himself was now of an age to begin thinking of a quiet retirement. According to the charter, Æthelmær himself was to live in the monastery, "like a father to the monks." Ælfric is mentioned in the charter, though not by name: "And I desire that he who is now the superior may continue to hold that office as long as he lives, and after his death that the brethren may choose one from their own number according as the rule prescribes, and I myself will live with them, and enjoy the endowment as long as life lasts." Ælfric himself witnessed the charter, along with fifteen other abbots.

After eighteen years of teaching and writing at Cernel, then,

Ælfric became an abbot himself, carrying on in a new role the work of the reform. The main structure of his work was complete now; the works that he wrote during this last period of his life were principally amplifications of that structure and "occasional pieces" written in his capacity as a well-known scholar-cleric.

An important group of these occasional pieces is the letters. A letter in Latin, *Letter to the Monks of Eynsham,* survives which was written as he began his abbacy. Another, in English, is the *Letter to Wulfgeat.* Wulfgeat of Ylmandun, a prominent landowner in the vicinity of Eynsham, was the son of Leofsige, ealdorman of the West Saxons; his name appears on a number of charters between 986 and 1005. In 1006, he was stripped, for some reason, of his honors and estates by a royal judgment. Ælfric refers in the brief introductory lines of the *Letter* to the English writings he had lent to Wulfgeat and to his promise to send more. In the first half of the *Letter,* which consists of a brief summary of basic Christian doctrine, Ælfric begins by describing the Trinity and then presents the Christian world-view from the Creation and the Fall of Man, through the Incarnation, to the Day of Judgment. The second half is a commentary, derived from Augustine, on the text, "Agree with thine adversary quickly, whiles thou art with him in the way" (Matthew 5:25).

The tone of Ælfric's lines to Wulfgeat suggests the position that Ælfric now had among the prominent laymen of the area. Similar in this respect is the *Letter to Sigeweard* that Ælfric wrote at the request of another prominent thane, Sigeweard of Easthealon. Sigeweard was one of those who had signed the Eynsham charter; Ælfric had visited his estate, as we know from a passage near the end of the work addressed to him. Ælfric says:

> Ðu woldest me laðian, þa ic wæs mid þe, þæt ic swiðor drunce swilce for blisse ofer minum gewunan: ac wite þu, leof man, þæt se þe oðerne neadað ofer his mihte to drincenne, þæt se mot aberan begra gilt, gif him ænig hearm of þam drence becymð. Ure Hælend Crist on his halgan godspelle forbead þone oferdrenc eallum gelyfdeum mannum: healde se ðe wille his gesetnysse.

> (When I was at your house you urged me to drink more than I was accustomed. You ought to know, dear friend, that if any one compels another to drink more than is good for him, and any harm result, the blame is upon him who caused it. Our Savior Christ in His gospel has forbidden believers to drink more than is necessary. Let him who will, keep the law of Christ.)
>
> (Crawford, 14–15)

The *Letter to Sigeweard* is interesting both as one of the fullest of Ælfric's several summaries of Christian doctrine, as he saw it, and as one of the few works which is basically original with him, though he did draw incidentally upon Augustine's *De Doctrina Christiana* and upon Isidore of Seville's *In Libros Veteris ac Novi Testamenti Proemia.* Caroline L. White characterizes the *Letter* as a "practical, historical introduction to the Holy Scriptures."[29] As Ælfric surveys the books of the Bible, he emphasizes the continuity of Scripture and the way that each book fits into sacred history. Beginning with the creation of the world, the fall of the angels, and the fall of man, he progresses through the history of Israel, the wisdom books, and the major and minor prophets. The second part of the book takes up the New Law: the gospels and epistles, the Acts, and the Revelation of John.

The *Letter to Sigefyrð* seems to be addressed to a local person, also. A Sigefyrð signed the Eynsham charter; perhaps he is the same thane to whom the *Letter* is addressed. The occasion which elicited the *Letter* is specified in the introduction:

Ælfric abbod gret Sigefyrð freondlice!
Me is gesæd, þæt þu sædest be me,
þæt ic oðer tæhte on Engliscum gewritum,
oðer eower ancor æt ham mid eow tæhð,
forþan þe he swutelice sægð, þæt hit sy alyfed,
þæt mæssepreostas wel moton wifian,
and mine gewritu wiðcweðað þysum.

(Ælfric, abbot, sends friendly greetings to Sigefyrð!
It was told to me that you said of me,
that I taught one thing in my English writings,
and the anchorite on your manor teaches another,
for he says openly that it is allowed
for priests to marry,
and my writings deny this.)

(Assmann, 13)

There follows a straightforward and detailed presentation of the argument for clerical chastity. Christ chose a maiden to be His mother, both He and His apostles lived chastely, as did the holy confessors of more recent times: Martin, Gregory, Augustine, Basil, Cuthbert, Bede, Jerome, and the desert fathers. Ælfric later revised this *Letter,* dropping the address to Sigefyrð and greatly expanding the discourse on chastity to make it a full homily (*De Virginitate* in CCCC 419).

The *Letters for Wulfstan* were written in response to a specific request from Ælfric's fellow homilist, Archbishop Wulfstan of York. Wulfstan was also Bishop of Worcester, near Ælfric's new monastery at Eynsham. About 1005, he asked Ælfric to write two letters in Latin on clerical duties to be used among the secular clergy; a year later, he asked him to translate these letters into English. The letters take up some of the same subjects as the similar letter which Wulfsige had commissioned from Ælfric a few years earlier. The first letter summarizes the Christian ages of the world, a familiar theme in Ælfric, as we have seen: the ages before the Law, under the Law, and under God's grace. He then describes the early church, the Roman persecutions, and the work of the synods. A list of the seven orders of the ministry follows, and the letter ends with a brief treatment of a priest's duties and obligations.

The second letter seems intended for use at an annual gathering of the clergy for the distribution of holy oil. It begins,

> *Eala ge mæssepreostas, mine gebroðra!*
> *We secgað eow nu þæt we ær ne sædon.*
> *Forþon þe we todæg sceol dalan urne ele,*
> *on þreo wisan gehalgodne, swa swa us gewisað seo boc . . . .*
> *halige ele, oþer his crisma and seocra manna ele.*
>
> *(O ye priests, my brothers!*
> *We say to you now what we have not said before.*
> *For today we are to divide our oil,*
> *hallowed in three ways, as the book tells us . . . .*
> *holy oil, chrism, and sick men's oil.)* (Fehr, 147)

The letter that follows gives directions for the administration of the Lord's Supper; the celebration of Passion Week, including Ash Wednesday and Palm Sunday; and the celebration of the Mass on other occasions. The letter also includes expositions of the Ten Commandments and the eight deadly sins. One version of this second English letter for Wulfstan is of particular interest, because it is Wulfstan's rewriting of Ælfric's work. Comparison of Wulfstan's version with Ælfric's original demonstrates very vividly the difference in their styles.

Finally, we may include among these "occasional pieces" Ælfric's Latin *Life of Æthelwold*. This *Life* was completed in 1006, for it is dedicated to Bishop Kenulph, who became Bishop of Winchester in 1006 and died the same year. The preface to the *Life* begins, "Ælfric abbot, an alumnus of Winchester, desires for the honorable Bishop Kenulph and the brethren of Winchester salvation in Christ. It seems to me worthy now at last to call to mind some of the deeds of our father and great teacher, Æthelwold, for twenty years have passed since his departure. With my narrative, brief indeed and unadorned, I gather into this writing those things which I have learned either from you or from other faithful ones, lest perchance they pass into utter oblivion for want of writers" (*V.Æ.*, 253).

The *Life of Æthelwold* was formerly generally thought to be an original work; it now appears to be a characteristically Ælfrician reworking of an earlier life by Wulfstan, a monk of Winchester.[30] This perhaps explains the almost complete absence of any personal reminiscences of Æthelwold and the highly conventional tone of the whole *Life*. (The preface itself, which does not mention any source specifically, is little more than a pastiche of the rhetorical clichés for the opening of a saint's life, such as the declaration that the knowledge of the saint is in danger of being lost, the assertion of personal knowledge, and the claim of a "rustic" style. It therefore proves little about the actual circumstances of composition.)

Through these active years as abbot, Ælfric not only responded to requests for works, he also continued to revise and augment his major work, his series of homilies. According to Clemoes's reconstruction of the chronology, the completion of the second series of Temporale Homilies belongs to these years, earlier works were reworked and reissued, and *Catholic Homilies* II, there is reason to believe, was revised and issued again. Separate pieces include the largely unpublished *De Creatore et Creature* and *De Sex Aetatibus Mundi,* which together present an "epitome of world history . . . which is very close to the main theme of Ælfric's total plan."[31]

The date of Ælfric's death is unknown. It used to be often given as about 1020, but on very scanty evidence; no documentary evidence exists to prove that Ælfric must have been alive in any given year after 1006. Clemoes suggests a date as early as 1010, on the basis of Ælfric's known works and the assumption of "an output at the same rate after 1006 as before it."[32] If he died then, he was about fifty-five years old.

CHAPTER 2

Catholic Homilies

WITH the following words, Ælfric, about 989, dedicated his first major work, *Catholic Homilies,* a volume of forty sermons freely translated from Latin into English prose:

> I, Ælfric, scholar of Æthelwold, the benevolent and venerable Superior, send greeting of good wishes to his Lordship Archbishop Sigeric in the Lord. However rashly or presumptuously undertaken, I have nevertheless formed this book out of Latin writers and from Holy Scripture, translating into our ordinary speech, for the edification of the simple, who know only this language both for reading and for hearing; and for that reason I have used no difficult words, but only plain English; so that our message might the more readily reach the hearts of those who read or hear, to the profit of the souls of those who cannot be taught in any other tongue than that to which they were born. (*CH* I, p. 1)

Later in this Latin preface, he states his intentions of supplying some of the omissions of "sermons or histories" in this first volume by issuing a second volume, already under preparation. This second series of homilies appeared in 992, again with a dedication to the Archbishop: "Inasmuch as you have only too amply praised the result of my study, and have willingly accepted that translation, I have hastened to form this following book, according as the grace of God has guided me (*CH* II, p. 1).

The Latin prefaces to the *Catholic Homilies* make very explicit Ælfric's immediate purpose in preparing these two volumes of sermons. He is first of all concerned to provide for the "unlearned of our race" knowledge for the salvation of their souls. He therefore has written in English, "avoiding garrulous verbosity and strange expressions, and seeking rather with pure and plain words, in the language of their nation, to be of use to my hearers, by simple speech, than to be praised for the composition of skillful discourse, which my simplicity has never acquired" (*CH* II, p. 1). At the same time, he is concerned that the doctrine, though understandable to the laity, be sound and orthodox. He lists his major authorities—

Augustine, Jerome, Bede, Gregory the Great, Smaragdus, and Haymo—and points out that "the authority of these writers is willingly accepted by all Catholics." He has, he says, "carefully avoided falling into errors that might lead astray," and he admonishes any who are dissatisfied with his work to make their own and not to "pervert my translation, which I trust by the grace of God, and not from vainglory, I have been able to work out by careful study." Lastly, as Clemoes has pointed out,[1] the prefaces indicate that Ælfric thought of his work as a "consciously 'literary' act." No doubt much of his work had been written to meet his own day-to-day needs as teacher and preacher, but these volumes are not random compilations of occasional pieces. They are the product of systematic thought and were offered to his superior and to the church as finished works. They may, therefore, be studied as unified wholes.

I *Contents and Arrangement*

The manuscripts of the two sets of Ælfric's homilies all bear the title *Sermones Catholici.* The title *Catholic Homilies* was assigned them by the seventeenth-century scholar Abraham Wheloc,[2] because they were intended for general, not merely monastic, use. In some respects, the manuscript label is more appropriate; for, strictly speaking, a "homily" is an exposition or a commentary on a scriptural text, a "sermon," a general discourse on a dogmatic or moral theme. About two-thirds of the items in the two volumes are homiletic, in the strict sense; the rest are narratives, topical discourses, or simple expansions of scriptural texts.

The first volume of *Catholic Homilies* contains, as Ælfric indicates in the preface, forty homilies that are arranged according to the feast-days of the church year, beginning with Christmas and ending with the second Sunday of Advent. The second volume, however, despite Ælfric's declaration in the preface to that volume, appears to contain forty-five homilies. This apparent contradiction has been resolved by Kenneth Sisam,[3] who has pointed out that *Catholic Homilies* II.XXIV and II.XXVII (here, as below, Benjamin Thorpe's numbering) are "pendants" to preceding sermons, and furthermore that the sermons numbered by Thorpe one through thirty-nine cover only thirty-four feast-days. The last six sermons are not assigned to specific days, but are for general use ("on the nativity of one apostle" and "on the dedication of a church"). The total number, reckoned by feast-days, is then the forty promised by Ælfric.

We have, therefore, eighty-five separate items: six general sermons for topical use, two "pendants," one sermon to be preached "whenever you will" and which serves as a general introduction to the two series (*CH* I.I), and seventy-six sermons arranged in two series which cover the major feast-days of the church year as observed by the English church. Ælfric says in his preface to the first volume that the division into two series is intended as a guard against tedium; and he suggests, as we have observed, that one series be read in church one year, the other the next. But he gives his permission for the two series to be combined into one, if anyone wishes to do so (*CH* I, p. 2). As a matter of fact, the earliest manuscripts of the homilies preserve Ælfric's division; later ones combine the sermons in both volumes into one sequence; and eventually, in other collections, the original integrity of the series is lost since the sermons are mixed indiscriminately with those of other authors.

The subjects of these sermons are as varied as their types. According to Smetana's reckoning,[4] of the eighty-five items, fifty-six are homiletic in the narrow sense; that is, they are commentaries on scriptural texts and are indebted to the Church Fathers. Seventeen others are saints' lives, and the remaining twelve are topical sermons, expansions of scriptural narrative, and so forth.

Partly because of Ælfric's free method of adaptation and partly because of the conventional nature of his material, the study of his sources for the sermons is a rather complicated matter.[5] The starting point is his own list of his major sources in his preface to Volume I: Augustine, Jerome, Bede, Gregory, Smaragdus, and Haymo. But relatively seldom does Ælfric produce a straightforward translation of a single text; almost invariably he weaves together, according to his own purposes, material from several sources, expanding and compressing source material and adding transitions and commentary of his own. For example, *Catholic Homilies* I.II draws on six separate homilies by Gregory, Smaragdus, and Bede; I.V and I.XXVII draw on five sources each; and II.III and II.V draw on four each.[6]

Ælfric's heaviest debts are to Gregory the Great, Bede, and Augustine, reflecting thereby his aim to make his homilies reflect the orthodox authority "willingly accepted by all Catholics." By a rough reckoning, Gregory is a major source for about thirty-three of the eighty-five items in the two volumes; Bede for about twenty-three; and Augustine for about fourteen. All three are used incidentally and for short passages here and there throughout other homilies as well; thus, the total work is permeated with the thought of these three Fathers. Although no other sources are used as pervasively as these three, many others are used: besides Jerome, Smaragdus, and Haymo (named in the preface), Severianus, Fulgentius, Ratramus, Origen, Sulpicius Severus, and various anonymous writers contribute major parts of one or more sermons.

A recent study of Ælfric's sources by Father Cyril Smetana has not only revealed some interesting facts about Ælfric's methods but indirectly provided some additional insight into his conceptions of his work.[7] Ælfric, he proves, used as his primary immediate source for the *Catholic Homilies* an already existing homiliary collected by Paul the Deacon. Paul the Deacon (720–799?) was a monk of Monte Cassino who spent some time at the court of Charlemagne, seeking the release of his brother who had been taken prisoner by the Frankish king. At Charlemagne's request, he compiled and edited an authoritative collection of nearly two hundred and fifty homilies for use in the Carolingian lands. This homiliary was regarded in its day as a masterpiece of critical scholarship and acquired enormous prestige. Versions and modifications of it remained in use for centuries, and its influence is still to be seen in the present calendar of feasts.

The list of items which comprise the original version of Paul's collection has been reconstructed by F. Wiegand.[8] On the basis of this list, Smetana has discovered that Ælfric was clearly heavily indebted to this homiliary. For the fifty-six exegetical homilies in Ælfric's collection, eighty-six patristic sources were used. Sixty-five of these appeared in the original version of Paul the Deacon's collection; most of the rest of them were in later versions of the work. It seems, therefore, that Ælfric had before him a version of the homiliary of Paul the Deacon very much like the original but varying from it in some respects.

Ælfric's use of Paul the Deacon not only underscores his emphasis on orthodoxy and authority in the prefaces but also tells us something of the way he conceived his task. Clemoes has pointed out the similarities in Paul's and Ælfric's projects.[9] Paul had compiled his collection in order to provide the basis for sound preaching in Charlemagne's realm. Ælfric had a similar aim for his own collection, which was written for use in an English church badly in need of learning and a sense of order. Paul's collection was requested by Charlemagne and received his approval; Ælfric similarly sought the official approval of Archbishop Sigeric, head of the English church, for his collection. In one important respect, however, Ælfric's aims went beyond those of Paul the Deacon. Whereas Paul had merely assembled patristic homilies in Latin, Ælfric reshaped his sources and put them into the language of his own country. The result was a carefully organized summary of the religious learning of his day, but Ælfric made it thoroughly English and at the same time Catholic in its authority and orthodoxy.

Paul the Deacon's collection was not the only source of this kind used by Ælfric, though it was the major one. He also drew upon collections by two other Carolingians, Smaragdus and Haymo of Auxerre, both specifically mentioned by Ælfric in his preface.[10] Smaragdus was the compiler of a series of brief excerpts from the works of the Fathers; Haymo, upon whose work Ælfric drew more heavily, had compiled a homiliary similar to Paul the Deacon's, though smaller in scope. Over twenty-five of the *Catholic Homilies* are indebted to some degree to Haymo's compilation. A fourth compilation, perhaps not really comparable, upon which Ælfric drew, was one he had made himself, a collection of items he apparently began to assemble even before he left Winchester and which survives in an eleventh-century copy now at Boulogne.[11] At least one item in this "commonplace book," a digest of Julian of Toledo's *Prognosticon,* furnished some details for the first volume of the *Catholic Homilies.*

Ælfric, as we shall see, handled his sources very freely. He often combined parts of several homilies and added material of his own to produce, in effect, a new work; but he always did so with a keen respect for the spirit of his authorities. But much of his attitude toward his work is suggested by his very selection of sources. His collection of homilies was not a random assemblage of occasional pieces; it was grounded upon a systematic selection of sources sanctioned not only by the authority of their authors but also by the approval of previous editors.

II *Ælfric's Methods of Interpretation*

Fifty-six, or approximately two-thirds, of the eighty-five sermons in the *Catholic Homilies* are exegetical: methodical expositions and commentaries on scriptural texts. In these homilies, Ælfric expounded his texts in accordance with a long, well-established tradition of exegesis. His translations of his sources are seldom mechanical or literal—he translated, he says, not "word for word" but "sense for sense"—but for the most part he adopts his sources' interpretations of scriptural texts without substantial alteration. In this fidelity to authority, he reflects, of course, his general intention of providing a body of orthodox doctrine in accessible form.

The basis of this exegetical method was the theory of allegory or multiple levels of meaning: the so-called fourfold (sometimes threefold) method of interpretation.[12] Apparently, this critical method is derived ultimately from Jewish haggadic exegesis, as adapted by Alexandrian philosophers and theologians in their effort to reconcile Christianity and Platonic philosophy. The most notable early figure in the tradition was the Alexandrian Neoplatonist Philo (c. 20 B.C.—c. 50 A.D.), who attempted to prove that Greek philosophical ideas underlay the story of the Old Testament. Philo drew not only upon Jewish traditions of allegory but also upon the Stoics' allegorical readings of Homer to construct a critical theory of multiple senses.

Philo's methods were taken over and refined by the third-century Christian theologian Origen. Origen fixed the outlines of the allegorical method for Christian writers, and his methods were followed, with some variations, to the end of the Middle Ages. Origen used a three-level system of interpretation: literal, moral, and spiritual. Essentially, this meant that any scriptural text could be interpreted as a literal statement, as a guide to morality, and as an allegorical allusion to the spiritual world. St. Augustine (354–430) used an adaptation of this scheme, which he explained in his *Of Christian Doctrine*. It incorporated four levels: historical (the literal level), etiological (consideration of causes), analogical (consideration of the relationship between the Old and New Testaments), and allegorical (a figurative level).

Ælfric's chief authority, Gregory the Great (c. 540–604), used a threefold method, much like Origen's, which Gregory explained in his dedication to his lectures on the Book of Job: "First we lay the foundations in history; then by following a symbolical sense, we erect an intellectual edifice to be a stronghold of faith; and lastly, by the grace of moral instruction, we as it were paint the fabric in fair colors.... For the word of God both exercises the understanding of the wise by its deep mysteries, and also by its superficial lessons nurses the simple-minded. It presents openly that wherewith the little ones may be fed; it keeps in secret that whereby men of loftier range may be rapt in admiration."[13] These three levels—literal, allegorical, and moral—with a fourth, the anagogical (dealing with the other world, the spiritual dimension, and Heaven and Hell) frequently added, became the standard model for the patristic exegetes; and it is followed by Ælfric.[14]

In practice, three kinds of figurative interpretations may be identified—allegory (in the strict sense), symbolism, and typology. Allegorical interpretations are usually *ad hoc* figurative readings of texts; symbolism, in contrast, is highly conventional and depends upon a body of traditional lore concerning the proper interpretation of, for example, numbers, animals, and plants. Each number in the Bible had a "deeper meaning." Key numbers, of course, were one (for the unity of God), three (for the Trinity), four (for the Evangelists), seven (for the sevenfold gifts of the Holy Spirit, the seven last words of Christ, the seven joys of Mary), and twelve (for the twelve tribes of Israel, the twelve disciples). But other numbers were also interpreted (two, for the love of God for man; five, for the Pentateuch), and the digits of a number were often added to provide additional material for interpretation. In the other large bodies of conventional symbolism, ones dealing with plants and animals, the lamb symbolized purity; the ram, power; the goat, lust; and the dove, meekness. The wolf was the devil. The palm, of course, indicated victory; the red rose, death; and the white lily, purity.

Typology was the interpretation of the Old Testament in the light of the New. The persons and events of the Old Testament were presumed to "prefigure" the life of Christ and the history and doctrines of the Catholic Church. Christ himself was "prefigured" in, among others, Adam, Noah, Moses, and Samson. Noah's ark, Eve, and the tabernacle all were types of the Church, while the Pharaoh was one of several types of the devil.

Ælfric took over from his models these arts of interpretation and bodies of lore, although he used them critically and with considerable sensitivity to the needs and capacities of his audience.

Of Christ's miracles, for example, he wrote in the sermon for Shrove Sunday,

Þeahhwæðere þa wundra þe Crist worhte, oðer ðing hi æteowdon þurh mihte, and oðre ðing hi getacnodon þurh geryno. He worhte þa wundra soðlice þurh godcunde mihte, and mid þam wundrum þæs folces geleafan getrymde; ac hwæðre þær was oðer ðing dingle on ðam wundrum, æfter gastlicum andgite.

(But the miracles which Christ wrought demonstrated one thing through power and another thing they betokened through mystery. He wrought these miracles truly through divine power, and with these miracles confirmed the people's faith; but yet there was another thing in those miracles, in a spiritual sense.) (*CH* I.X, 154)

This contrast between the literal and the spiritual senses Ælfric often expressed as between the "lichamlic" or "flæsclic" and the "gastlic." He uses a small number of other formulas to introduce allegorical interpretations. A typical example is the following from the sermon for Midlent Sunday:

Ac we willaþ eow secgan þæt gastlic andgit þyssera ealdra gesetnyssa, forþan þe seo ealde æ is mid gastlicum andgyte afylled. . . .

(But we will say to you the spiritual sense of these old institutes, for the old law is filled with spiritual meaning. . . .) (*CH* II.XII, 198)

The potentialities for excess in the use of the allegorical method are obvious. Ælfric, who often declines to follow his sources into the most strained interpretations, either merely omits them silently or gives as his reason the limitations of his hearers:

Þises godspelles traht precð gyt menigfealdlicor ymb ðas wæter-fatu and heora getacnungum, ac we ondraedað us þæt ge ðas foresædan getacnunga to gymeleaste doð, gif we eow swiðor be ðam gereccað.

(The exposition of this gospel speaks yet more fully about these water-vessels and their meanings, but we fear that you will neglect the meanings already given, if we relate to you further about them.) (*CH* II.IV, 70)

Professor Schelp cites an amusing example of Ælfric's conservatism of interpretation of numbers.[15] Gregory, in his Homily 24, grapples with the fact that Peter is said to have caught 153 fish (John 21:11). This is the number of the elect, Gregory says, and is the product of adding the Ten Commandments to the Sevenfold Gifts and multiplying twice by the Trinity ($10 + 7 \times 3 \times 3 = 153$). This, apparently, is too much for Ælfric, and he omits it, remarking merely:

> Ða getel þæra fixa hæfþ maran getacnunge þonne ge understandan magon.
>
> (The number of the fishes has a greater tokening than you can understand.) (*CH* II.XVII, 292)

Allegorical interpretation is, of course, not the only method used by Ælfric. He also frequently uses classification, for example, and he is a master of the exemplum, or illustrative story. He is a critical follower of tradition, also, in the larger structural patterns of his homilies. He regularly uses the method called "continuous gloss": the arrangement of text and gloss consecutively, as opposed to placing the gloss in the margin or between the lines of the text. Thus a homily often consists of a biblical text, followed by a section of doctrine, in which the text is thoroughly glossed, and finally a moral section which points the lesson for the audience.[16]

Ælfric's use of traditional methods of exegesis and his critical conservatism in following his sources, like his selection of the sources themselves, indicate his desire to build a body of preaching materials for the laity which would be beyond reproach in their permanent relevance and authority.

III *Homiletic Exegesis: Midlent Sunday*

The twelfth sermon of the first series, for Midlent Sunday, may serve to illustrate Ælfric's customary method of developing an exegetical sermon. Not one of his most inspired sermons, it is however, fairly typical of this kind of sermon; furthermore, it contains some interesting remarks on the art of interpretation itself. Ælfric's text is Matthew's account of the miracles of the loaves and the fishes. He begins with a graceful English translation of the text itself, telling how Christ went to the sea of Galilee and to a mountain with his disciples ("leorning-cnihta") and was followed by five thousand people. Calling for a little boy's five barley loaves and two fishes, he blessed them and divided them among the five thousand and "hi ealle genoh hæfdon" (they all had enough). And what was left over filled twelve baskets. Having set forth the text, Ælfric proceeds to interpret it line by line, drawing upon various arts of interpretation. The sea is interpreted allegorically as the world, and Christ's passing over it reminds us that Christ came into this world as a man. He ascended the mountain and sat with His disciples as He ascended to heaven and sits now with the saints. The sea is an appropriate figure for this world, Ælfric says, because of its variety and changeable nature.

Christ's lifting up His eyes and seeing the multitude coming is also interpreted allegorically as His receiving those who come to Him spiritually. He will feed these with "gastlicum fodan" (spiritual food) as He fed the multitude with the loaves and the fishes. Ælfric now comes to the miracle itself, and he inserts some characteristic comments on miracles. Although Ælfric does not minimize the miraculous either in his homilies or in his saints' lives, he nevertheless often reveals a certain wariness about emphasizing them too much and takes pains to equate them with the normal order of things. Thus, here:

> Fela wundra worhte God, and dæghwamlice wyrcð; ac ða wundra sind swiðe awacode on manna gesihðe, forðon ðe hi sind swiðe gewunelice. Mare wundor is þæt God Ælmihtig ælce dæg fet ealne middangeard, and gewissað þa godan, þonne þæt wundor wære, þæt he þa gefylde fif ðusend manna mid fif hlafum: ac ðæs wundredon men, na forði þæt hit mare wundor wære, ac forði þæt hit wæs ungewunelic.
>
> (God has wrought many miracles and daily works; but these miracles are much weakened in the sight of men, because they are very common. A greater miracle it is that God Almighty every day feeds all the world, and directs the good, than that miracle was, that he filled five thousand men with five loaves: but men wondered at this, not because it was a greater miracle, but because it was unusual.) (*CH* I.XII, 184)

Ælfric then indicates the necessity of interpretation of written texts. With a picture, it is enough to see it and praise it, but a story is often "deope on getacnungum" (deep in its significations):

> Swa is eac on ðam wundre þe God worhte mid þam fif hlafum: ne bið na genoh þæt we þæs tacnes wundrian, oþþe þurh þæt God herian, buton we eac þæt gastlice andgit understandon.

(So also it is with regard to the miracle which God wrought with the five loaves: it is not enough that we wonder at the miracle, or praise God on account of it, without also understanding its spiritual sense.)

(*CH* I.XII, 186)

Ælfric uses allegory and plant and number symbolism to set forth the "spiritual sense" of the miracle. The loaves and fishes stand for Christ's teaching, and He gives the food to His disciples to distribute, just as He sent them later into the world to teach His doctrine. The leftover scraps suggest the deeper doctrines which the laity cannot understand and which the clergy must gather and preserve. The boy who brought the bread and fish, because he did not taste it himself, suggests the Jewish people who did not understand their scriptures until Christ revealed their meaning.

Each number has its significance, in conformity with tradition and with the general interpretation of the text. The five loaves are the five books of the Pentateuch, but the two fishes symbolize the Psalms and the Prophets. There were five thousand men in the crowd to correspond to the five loaves; and, because a thousand is a "perfect number," it suggests the perfection of those fed by Christ's teachings. The twelve baskets into which the fragments were gathered stand for the twelve disciples, who received those doctrines of Christ which were too difficult for the laity. Plant symbolism is used to gloss the detail that the multitude sat upon the grass. Since "all flesh is grass," grass conventionally means "fleshly desire"; and those fed by Christ must trample and press down fleshly desires as the multitude sat upon the grass.

His doctrinal section completed, with the text thoroughly glossed, Ælfric concludes his tripartite structure with a moral section of admonition to his audience. The multitude declared Jesus to be a prophet after seeing his miracle; we will be blessed if, not having seen, we still believe:

We cweðað nu, mid fullum geleafan, þæt Crist is soð witega, and ealra witegena Witega, and þæt he is soðlice ðæs Ælmihtigan Godes Sunu, ealswa mihtig swa his Fæder, mid ðam he leofað and rixað on annysse ðæs Halgan Gastes, a buton ende on ecnysse. Amen.

(We say now, with full belief, that Christ was a true prophet, and prophet of all prophets, and that he is truly Son of the Almighty God, as mighty as his Father, with whom he lives and reigns in unity of the Holy Ghost, ever without end to eternity. Amen.)

(*CH* I. XII, 190, 192)

The Midlent homily is based on two homilies by Augustine and Bede, and the interpretation of the miracle of the loaves and the fishes is thoroughly traditional. If it seems strained and pedantic to a modern reader, it is because we have lost the medieval perception of the world as suffused with the mystery of God and of sacred literature as a pleasingly enigmatic store of layered meaning. Ælfric, of course, shared these perceptions with his authorities; he uses their interpretation of the miracle and then weaves it into a clear and graceful presentation of his own, appropriate to his audience.

IV *Homiletic Narrative: The Vision of Drihthelm*

About seventeen of the items in the *Catholic Homilies* are saints' lives as Ælfric promised in the Latin preface to the first series; "And I have not only explained the writings of the Evangelists in this work, but have also set forth the life and passions of saints, for the benefit of the unlearned of our race" (*CH* I, p. 1). In the first series appear lives of St. Stephen (III), St. John (IV), St. Clement the Martyr (XXXVII), and St. Andrew (XXXVIII). In the second series appear St. Stephen again (II); St. Gregory the Great (IX); St. Cuthbert (X); St. Benedict (XI); SS. Philip and James (XVIII); SS. Alexander, Eventius, and Theodolus (XX); St. Fursey (XXII); the Vision of Drihthelm (XXIII); St. James the Apostle (XXXI); the Seven Sleepers (XXXII); St. Matthew (XXXVII); SS. Simon and Jude (XXXVIII); and St. Martin (XXXIX).

Ælfric's sources for these hagiological sermons are varied. Some are taken over from already existing sermon treatments, as are the sermons on St. Stephen; others are adapted from longer accounts, such as Sulpicius Severus's Life of St. Martin; while still others are based on non-hagiological works, like the sermons on the vision of Drihthelm and the story of Ymma, which are drawn from Bede's *Ecclesiastical History*.[17]

The homiletic saints' lives in the *Catholic Homilies* celebrate saints commemorated by the whole Church. The *Lives of Saints* collection was to deal with the saints which the monks commemorated among themselves, and it was apparently intended primarily for private reading rather than for liturgical use. This distinction, as we shall see, is a rather fine one; and the items in the *Lives of Saints* are similar in form to those in the *Catholic Homilies*. But it is worthwhile to look briefly at one of the earlier narratives which was intended directly for homiletic presentation to a lay audience. And a good example for this purpose is Ælfric's treatment of "The Vision of Drihthelm," both because of its intrinsic interest and because it typifies Ælfric's ordinary practice in adapting a narrative to homiletic use. The "Vision" (*CH* II.XXIII) is very closely based on Bede's *Ecclesiastical History* (V.12), as Ælfric acknowledges in the opening lines of the homily:

> Beda, ure lareow, awrat, on ðære bec þe is gehaten "Historia Anglorum," be sumes mannes æriste, on ðisum iglande, þisum wordum writende:
>
> (Bede, our doctor, has written, in the book which is called "Historia Anglorum," of a certain man's resurrection in this island, in these words writing:)
>
> (*CH* II. XXIII, 348)

The item is headed *Alia Visio* (Another Vision), and its selection was obviously suggested by the preceding item, an adaptation of the anonymous "Life of Fursey." Fursey was a Scottish priest who twice visited the underworld and had angels and devils war over possession of his soul. He remained unharmed except for a burn on the shoulder and face, a reminder of a minor misdeed; and, after his second return, he spent twelve years going around Britain, telling his story, and exhibiting his burn.

The stories of Fursey and Drihthelm are, of course, chiefly interesting today as specimens of the popular medieval literary form, the visit to the underworld, a form which serves as the basis of Dante's *The Divine Comedy*. The "Vision of Drihthelm," though much shorter and simpler than Fursey's vision, shares many of its characteristics: the presence of a heavenly guide, a fiery vision, and comments on the transformed later life of the visionary. Drihthelm is said to have been a pious Northumbrian who rose from his deathbed the morning after his death. He divided his property among his wife, his children, and the poor and entered the monastery at Melrose.

The bulk of the story is Drihthelm's own account of his experience. He was led by a shining angel to a vast, burning pit where he saw lost souls being tormented; among them were five new arrivals, including a priest, a layman, and a woman. He was then led eastward to a beautiful, flowery place, which he was told was Heaven, and then returned to his body. After his return, he led a life of great asceticism, often praying while standing up to his neck in an icy stream:

Ðaða hine man axode hu he mihte ðone micclan cyle forberan, he andwyrde, "Maran cyle ic geseah, and wyrsan." Eft, ðaða hi axoden hu he mihte swa stearce forhæfednysse healdan, he andwyrde, "Stiðran and wyrsan ic geseah."

(When any one asked him how he could bear that great cold, he answered, "I have seen a greater and worse cold." Again, when they asked him how he could observe such rigid abstinence, he answered, "I have seen a more rigid and worse.")

(*CH* II.XXIII, 254)

Bede's treatment of the story of Drihthelm is of an appropriate length for a homily, and Ælfric translates it fairly straightforwardly with few omissions and no expansions. He does omit Bede's circumstantial details of Drihthelm's home and of Melrose and his historically-minded account of his authority for the story, a monk named Hæmgils who had known Drihthelm. He also alters the sequence of Bede's narrative to provide a dramatic situation for Drihthelm's account of his vision. Bede mentions near the end of the account that King Aldfrith used to visit Drihthelm; Ælfric introduces this episode earlier and makes the vision a dramatic speech to Aldfrith and "certain pious men."

But these are minor changes. Ælfric also adds a brief conclusion, citing a similar vision in Gregory's *Dialogues* and pointing the obvious lessons: that we must live piously and seek to help those in hell-torment through our prayers. The homily is interesting not because of its striking interpretations or any particular originality in treatment but because it exemplifies Ælfric's keen sense of his audience's attention, his perception of homiletic possibilities in a non-homiletic source, and the clarity and economy of his handling of narrative. We also see these characteristics illustrated in the narratives of the *Lives of Saints*.

V *Moral Instruction: On the Greater Litany*

To the categories of exegetical homilies and saints' lives in the *Catholic Homilies,* we may add a third, rather loose category of sermons of general moral instruction. All the sermons, of course, are filled with moral applications of doctrine; and Ælfric's customary sermon structure calls for a section of direct moral counsel at the conclusion. But a few of the sermons are not tied to a particular text or devoted to a narrative; they are devoted wholly to moral instruction. Such a sermon is the twenty-first item in the second series: "On the greater litany."

This sermon apparently is largely original with Ælfric.[18] Although various details may have been derived from his reading, the structure and organization seem to be his own. He begins with a characteristic statement that teachers have an obligation to transmit holy knowledge to those who are not learned, in order that men should not err through ignorance. He then quotes Christ's "highest commandment":

> Lufa ðinne Drihten mid ealre ðinre heortan, and mid eallum mode: þis is þæt mæste bebod. Is eft oðer bebod ðisum swiðe gelic, Lufa ðinne nextan swa swa ðe sylfne: þas twa bebodu belucað ealle bec.

> (Love thy Lord with all thine heart, and with all thy mind: this is the greatest commandment. There is again another commandment very like unto this, Love thy neighbor as thyself: these two commandments comprise all the books.)
>
> (*CH* II. XXI, 314)

The first half of the sermon is built around an exposition of this text. Ælfric proceeds by defining key words; first comes an examination of the meaning of "love." Christ and John are quoted to the effect that love is proved by good works, and the love of God and the love of man are contrasted and compared; then "neighbor" is examined, and Christ is quoted on the universal brotherhood of man. Through this first section of the sermon, Ælfric characteristically continually provides exempla, parables, and homely illustrations of his abstract points. On the presence of the Holy Trinity in men's hearts, he says:

> Menn dæftað heora hus, and wel gedreoglæcað, gif hi sumne freond onfon willað to him, þæt nan unðaeslicnys him ne ðurfe derian; and we sceolon us clænsian fram unclænum dædum, þæt se Mihtiga God on urum mode wunige, seðe ænne gehwilcne þurh his Gast geneosað.

> (Men put their houses in order, and are well content, if they desire to receive a friend to them, that no impropriety may offend him; and we should cleanse ourselves from unclean deeds, that the Mighty God may dwell in our mind, who visits every one through his Spirit.)
>
> (*CH* II.XVI, 316)

In the second part of the sermon, Ælfric turns to separate consideration of the moral obligations of the various classes of men from kings downward. The key virtues for kings are righteousness and wisdom, for they must first direct themselves and then their people. Bishops, priests, and judges are admonished to use their authority wisely and justly and to live in such a way as to exemplify their own teachings. The duties of wives and husbands, parents and children are the subject of a long section in which Ælfric takes up his favorite theme of chastity. The purpose of sexual intercourse is procreation, and lust is wrong, even within wedlock:

God forgeaf gescead menniscum gesceafte, and ungesceadwisum nytenum asetne timan, þæt men sceoldon lybban heora lif mid gesceade, swa swa ða clænan nytenu cepað heora timan. Se mann is gesceapen to his Scyppendes anlicnysse, and soðlice ða nytenu sindon sawullease. Nu bið mannum sceamu þæt hi mislybban sceolon, and ða nytenu healdað heora gesetnysse.

(God gave reason to the human creation, and to the irrational animals a fixed time, so that men might live their lives with reason, as the clean animals observe their times. Man is created in his Creator's likeness, and truly animals are soulless. Now it is a shame to men that they should mislive, and the animals observe their established law.)

(*CH* II.XXI, 324)

Parents are enjoined to correct their children and they in turn are to honor their parents, and a cautionary tale is told of a child who was recklessly nurtured. He cursed God, without parental reproof, until devils carried him off as he cried, "My father! My father!" Brief counsel is also given to servants and masters, to the rich and the poor, which leads Ælfric into a concluding section in which he generally considers the problem of the distribution of happiness and misery in the world. His conclusion is highly orthodox:

Menigfealde beoð þæs Metodan Drihtnes egsan and swingla ofer scyldigum mannum, þæt ða sceortan witu ðises geswincfullan lifes forcyttan ða toweardan, þe næfre ne ateoriað.

(Manifold are the Lord Creator's terrors and scourges over guilty men, in order that the short punishments of this painful life may prevent those to come, which will never fail.)

(*CH* II. XXI, 328)

VI *Ælfric as a Homilist*

As the comments on particular homilies have indicated, the eighty-five items in the two series of *Catholic Homilies* are varied in subject matter and in structure. Yet, it is possible to make some general comments on Ælfric's practices as a writer of homilies and thus to indicate something of the nature of his achievement in this area. First of all, the doctrine expressed in the homilies is highly orthodox; and it consists of the basic teachings of the church. In many respects, it is summarized in the first sermon in the double series, "On the Beginning of Creation," to be preached "whenever you will," which serves as a general introduction to the collection. This sermon begins by summarizing Genesis and then tells of the coming of Christ, His sacrifice, and His resurrection. The end of the homily extends the story to the last judgment, when "He shall come at the end of the world with great majesty, in clouds" (*CH* I. I, 28).

This Christian view of history contains the basic elements of Ælfric's doctrines, which are those of the church as a whole. He returns over and over to the same themes: God the Creator, the Trinity, the life and works of Christ, and man's sin and redemption. His moral teaching is similarly straightforward and orthodox. Favorite topics are the duties of priests and teachers to spread the word of God and those of priests and laymen alike to pursue the ideal of chastity, spiritual as well as fleshly. Taken as a whole, the two series of homilies amply fulfill Ælfric's promise in the Latin preface to the first series to provide knowledge "which I thought might be enough for simple persons, for the amendment of their lives, inasmuch as laymen cannot take in all things, though they may learn them from the mouth of the learned" (*CH* I, p. 1).

The treatment of this material is equally orthodox. As we have seen, Ælfric took care to select as his sources those writers universally approved by the church; not only in the prefaces but also within the individual sermons, he continually points out that his work is derived from established authority: "the wise Augustine," "the doctor Haymo," "Gregory the expounder." He follows their methods of interpretation—allegorical, typological, symbolic—and adopts, for the most part, their readings of the texts. Although his treatments of his sources would hardly be called "translation" today but "free adaptation," he preserves through his reorderings the interpretations of his authorities.

Although Ælfric's English prose style is considered in some detail in Chapter 6, we may note that the *Catholic Homilies,* though for the most part not in the fully developed rhythmic style of Ælfric's later works, are written in a style notable for its clarity and movement—one eminently suited to oral delivery. Indeed, perhaps the most notable feature of Ælfric's manner as a homilist is his continual sense of his audience's needs and capacities. His sources are extremely varied in style, length, and degree of complexity; but Ælfric transmutes each of them into a piece suited to the comprehension of his listeners. We are often reminded of this intent by the direct addresses to the listeners. In the sermon on the "Octaves and Circumcision of Our Lord," for example, he interrupts his exposition to say, "It is probable that some of you do not know what circumcision is" (*CH* I.VI, 92). And he then explains the meaning of the word, with comments on its history and spiritual significance. Or, when he feels it necessary to develop a theme at some length, he will insert a word of encouragement: "This is very wearisome for you to hear; if we had dared to pass it silently, we should not have said it to you" (*CH* II.XXI, 324).

But the real concern of Ælfric for his audience comes less from such direct comments as these than from the overall design of the series and Ælfric's control of that design. Structured inevitably around two progressions through the church calendar, the homilies present a comprehensive view of Christian history in a form both acceptable to the learned and accessible to the humble. In the care with which they are composed and in the larger purposes which they achieve, they go beyond their first purpose of supplying the immediate needs of a preacher to take on the qualities, in Clemoes's words, of a "consciously 'literary' act."

CHAPTER 3

Lives of Saints

ÆLFRIC introduced his *Lives of Saints,* a third collection of translations written about 998, with these words. (The dedication to Æthelweard is the chief evidence for the date, but since Æthelweard did not die until 1002, the collection may be that late.)

Ælfric gret eadmodlice Æþelwerd ealdorman, and ic secge þe, leof, þæt ic hæbbe nu gegaderod on þyssere bec þæra halgena þrowunga þe me to onhagode on englisc to awendene, for þan þe ðu, leof, swiðost, and Æðelmær, swylcera gewrita me bædon, and of handum gelæhton eowerne geleafan to getrymmenne mid þære gerecednysse þe ge on eowrum gereorde næfdon ær. Ðu wast, leof, þæt we awendon on þam twam ærrum bocum þæra halgena þrowunga and lif þe angelecynn mid freols-dagum wurþað. Nu geweard us þæt we þas boc be þæra halgena ðrowungum and life gedihton þe mynstermenn mid heora þenungum betwux him wurðiað.

(Ælfric greets humbly Æthelweard ealdorman, and I say to you, sir, that I have now gathered into this book such passions of the saints as I have had leisure to translate into English, because you, sir, and Æthelmær have most earnestly asked me for such writings, and from my hands you have already received, for the strengthening of your faith, writings which you never had before in your language. You know, sir, that we translated in the two earlier books the passions and lives of those saints which the English people honor with feast-days. Now it has seemed good to us to write this book about the passions and lives of those saints whom the monks celebrate among themselves.)

(*LS*, English Preface, 4)

In the six to ten years since the second series of *Catholic Homilies* had appeared, Ælfric had probably been at work on other pieces, including the *Grammar,* the *De Temporibus Anni,* and his Bible translations. There is a suggestion in the preface that Ælfric had been giving single lives to Æthelweard to read for some time before he gathered them into a set.

Much the best surviving manuscript of the *Lives* is the British Museum manuscript (Cotton Julius E. vii), from which W. W. Skeat printed his edition. Skeat numbered the separate items in his edition of this manuscript I through XXXVI. Four of these items have been shown to be not by Ælfric (XXIII, XXIIIB, XXX, and XXXIII),[1] and eight others are not saints' lives, but discourses on general subjects (I, XII, XIII, XV, XVI, XVII, XVIII, and XXV). Nevertheless, the headings in the manuscript are somewhat ambiguous and do not correspond exactly to Skeat's; and it seems that if the four non-Ælfrician items were dropped and the numbering altered, we would have a collection of forty items, parallel in this respect to each volume of the *Catholic Homilies.*[2] Despite Ælfric's statement in the preface and the general tenor of the collection, there is no reason to believe that the non-hagiological items were not originally part of the set.

The *Lives* have commonly been referred to as a third set of "homilies." It is true that they are comparable to the earlier series in form and arrangement; indeed, the two *Catholic Homilies* contain some hagiological homilies, as we have seen. However, as Clemoes has pointed out,[3] the *Lives* appear to be intended for private reading, not for liturgical use. The homilies regularly include oral formulas (such as "we will relate to you . . .") which are missing in the *Lives*. Furthermore, the items in the *Lives* are more varied in length and do not seem to be tied to the time requirements of preaching, as the homilies are (however loosely). Also, the *Lives* are explicitly intended for monastic use, and there is some question as to whether preaching would have been done in the vernacular to a monastic congregation at this time. The distinction may not be an important one. Obviously, the *Homilies* might be read privately; and the *Lives* might serve, and undoubtedly often did serve, as the bases of sermons.

The selection of material and the sources used in the *Lives of Saints* demonstrate aims similar to those for the *Catholic Homilies*. In the *Lives,* as in the *Homilies,* Ælfric is clearly pursuing his plan to provide a sound, systematic body of Christian literature for his country. The separate items are widely varied, but collectively they constitute a broad survey of the major individual saints and kinds of saints honored by the faithful. Two of the items, for example, are lives of apostles—number XV, on St. Mark, and number XXXVI, on St. Thomas the Apostle. The other apostles had been treated in the *Catholic Homilies;* Ælfric's comprehensive aims are clear by his inclusion of the last two in the *Lives*.

Of the eight items in the series that are not hagiographic, one—"The Memory of the Saints"—seems intended as a kind of general introduction to the series; it was perhaps originally placed first in the collection, though it is number XVI in Skeat's edition of the Cotton manuscript. Other non-hagiographic items include biblical material (XVIII, on the Book of Kings; XXV, on the Maccabees) and general discourses, such as XII, on Ash Wednesday, and XVII, "On Auguries."

The Roman martyrs constitute the subjects of the largest single group of lives. There are accounts of the "passions" of St. Julian (IV), St. Sebastian (V), the Forty Soldiers (XI), St. George (XIV), and half a dozen more. A particular kind of Roman martyr—the virgin martyr—is the subject of several of these lives. Another notable group deals with the lives of native English saints. Ælfric himself obviously was particularly interested in providing his audience with accounts of British saints; and he drew upon Bede and upon Latin hagiographers of his own day for lives of St. Alban (XIX), St. Æthelthryth (XX), St. Swithun (XXI), St. Oswald (XXVI), and St. Edmund (XXXII). Another large group consists of lives of famous "confessors," bishops and abbots who had attained sainthood not through martyrdom but through ecclesiastical service. Among these lives are those of St. Basilius (III); St. Maurus, missionary from St. Benedict to the Franks (VI); and St. Martin (XXXI).

The sources of the *Lives of Saints* cannot be described as easily as those of the *Catholic Homilies.*[4] No one writer is so dominant among them as Gregory is among the authorities for the *Homilies,* and the range of sources is very wide. As in the *Homilies,* though, Ælfric shows in *Lives of Saints* a careful concern for textual matters; and he selects the "standard" life of each saint for his translation. He uses, for instance, Ambrose's lives of St. Sebastian and St. Agnes, Sulpicius Severus's life of St. Martin, and Bede's accounts of the earlier English saints. A number of the lives are based upon versions of anonymous lives now gathered in the *Acta Sanctorum.*

However, despite the apparent intention in the *Lives* to represent the whole range of Latin hagiography and to draw upon standard sources, Ælfric does not include a number of lives that would seem to have been obvious choices: Jerome's life of Paul the Hermit, for example, and Athanasius's life of St. Anthony, which was widely known in the translation into Latin by Evagrius. Indeed, none of the lives of the "desert fathers" appears in the series. An explanation, of sorts, for this omission appears in the Latin preface to the *Lives:* "I hold my peace as to the book called *Vitae Patrum*, wherein are contained many subtle points which ought not to be laid open to the laity, nor indeed are we ourselves quite able to fathom them" (*LS*, Latin Preface, 2). What exactly Ælfric regarded as inappropriate for the laity in the *Vitae Patrum,* he does not explain. His comment is even more puzzling since he has just said that the book is intended for monks, not the laity; furthermore, it appears that he did draw upon some version of the *Vitae Patrum,* despite his apparent disclaimer.[5]

I *English Saints' Lives Before Ælfric*

Ælfric was by no means the first to write saints' lives in English; such pieces had been written in England at least as early as the latter part of the eighth century.[6] The great body of Latin hagiography had been introduced into England very soon after the conversion in 597 by missionaries eager to reinforce their teachings by providing their new converts with a spiritual substitute for the heroic legends of their pagan past. According to Bede, Gregory the Great sent relics to England; and, very early, churches were named after prominent saints. By the early eighth century, enough saints' lives were available in England for Bede to make an important contribution to the tradition by composing the first historical martyrology, one that gave not only names and dates but also a brief narrative of the circumstances of each martyr's death. Bede also wrote other hagiographic pieces, including two lives of St. Cuthbert, the *Lives of the Abbots,* and the many saints' lives embedded in the *Ecclesiastical History of the English Church and People.* Other writers, too, were at work on saints' lives at about the same time: an anonymous monk of Whitby had written a life of Cuthbert, and a monk of Lindisfarne had written the earliest life of Gregory the Great.

Bede and his contemporaries wrote their saints' lives in Latin; the first lives in English—at least among those that survive—seem to have been written in Mercia toward the end of the eighth century. There are six of these lives, in alliterative English verse: *Elene, Juliana, Fates of the Apostles, Andreas,* and two poems on St. Guthlac. (*Andreas* may not be Mercian in origin, but may be evidence of a Northumbrian school of English hagiographic verse.)

Of these poems, *Elene*, *Juliana*, and the *Fates of the Apostles* are the work of Cynewulf, on the evidence of runic "signatures" bearing his name. All of these poems are derived from Latin originals. Even the Guthlac poems, the only ones concerning a native saint, are based on an anonymous eighth-century Latin life of Guthlac. *Elene*, derived from the Latin *Acta Cyriaci,* concerns the discovery by Helena, the mother of Constantine, of the true cross. *Juliana*, a typical tale of the martyrdom of a virgin saint, is perhaps even more extravagantly told than its Latin source is. The brief, sub-literary *Fates of the Apostles* is a simple list of the ways the twelve apostles met their deaths. *Andreas* is a romantic tale of the adventures of St. Andrew and St. Matthew among the cannibal Anthropophagites, and the Guthlac poems are poetic treatments of episodes from the life of the English hermit. It is very likely that these six surviving poems are only a small part of the hagiographic material produced in England in the eighth century. There may well have been other poems of this kind, and it is almost certain that legends of the saints, especially local ones, must have been in oral circulation when Bede gathered the materials for his *History*.[7]

The works produced in Wessex in the late ninth century under the supervision of King Alfred did not include saints' lives, unless we may so term the *Dialogues* of Gregory the Great, translated by Bishop Werferth of Worcester. The second book of the *Dialogues* consists of a life of St. Benedict, and the fourth contains a number of legends of saints' visits to heaven and hell. A few scattered pieces suggest, however, that the writing of saints' lives in the vernacular did continue through this period. The ninth-century *Life of St. Chad*, written in Mercia, and the *Blickling Homilies*, probably written slightly earlier than Ælfric's, include several saints' lives. The *Life of Chad* and the *Blickling Homilies* are written in a heightened style, indebted to poetic practice; and they thus anticipate, in a general way, Ælfric's stylistic methods.

In short, enough vernacular saints' lives survive from the Old English period to suggest that, at least in the eighth and tenth centuries, many such lives must have been written, the bulk of which are now lost. Even on the basis of the surviving texts alone, Rosemary Woolf points out that "the hagiographic form was the dominant narrative kind in the Old English period."[8] There is nothing surprising in this fact; in some ways, the saint's life came to fill in a Christianized society the function that the epic or lay had had in pagan society; and we may see the epic manner appearing in many ways in the Cynewulfian saints' lives not only in diction but also in characterization and tone. The lurid sensationalism of *Juliana*, for example, must have had something of the same popular appeal as pagan tales of adventure had; and *Andreas* is very self-consciously indebted to *Beowulf*. A precedent already existed for the treatment of saints' lives in such secular and "literary" manners in the work of the fourth-century Prudentius, whose *Peristephanon* consists of verse accounts of the passions of fourteen martyrs.

Bede's hagiographic writings, the *Life of Chad*, and the *Blickling Homilies*, are most specifically religious in purpose. Bede wrote in Latin for the edification of a monastic audience; the *Life of Chad* and the *Blickling Homilies* are didactic in purpose, but they are in English and were probably intended for a lay audience. Their authors, like Ælfric, wrote to provide materials for sermons for the common people. In many ways, Ælfric's *Lives of Saints* is the epitome of several tendencies in Old English hagiography. Like the earlier vernacular homiletic saints' lives, his lives are intended to instruct; and, like the eighth-century hagiographic poems, they please by recalling the diction and the style of the heroic poems of the past, so that the Christian saints seem to be genuine heirs of the heroes of Germanic legend.

II *"The Memory of the Saints"*

Peter Clemoes has pointed out that number XVI in the *Lives of Saints* was probably originally intended to stand at the head of the collection as a sort of general introduction.[9] Like the *Lives of Saints*, both series of *Catholic Homilies* begin their sermons for specific dates with Christmas Day, the beginning of the church year. But the *Homilies* have an item outside this scheme which seems to serve as an introduction: "On the Beginning of Creation," to be preached "whenever you wish." "The Memory of the Saints" (XVI), which was probably intended to occupy a similar place in the *Lives of Saints*, is also marked "Spel loca hwænne mann wille" (to be preached when you will).

"The Memory of the Saints" is also closely parallel to "On the Beginning of Creation" in its form and method, and thus illuminates not only Ælfric's intentions in the *Lives* but also the relationship the series bears to the *Catholic Homilies* in Ælfric's overall plan.

Like "On the Beginning of Creation," the piece is a broad account of universal history. But whereas "On the Beginning of Creation" turns around the pivotal events in Christian history—the Creation, the Incarnation, the Last Judgment—"The Memory of the Saints" is appropriately built around the pivotal characters in the history. The *Lives of Saints*, it is suggested, is to deal with the same material as the *Catholic Homilies*; but the intent is to present this material through the lives of individual men.

The structure of the homily is based upon two of Ælfric's most frequently used rhetorical devices: classification and enumeration. The first half consists of a chronological roll-call of the categories of saints. We must take care to live piously, Ælfric says, and

We magon niman gode bysne,
ærest, be ðam halgum heah-fæderum,
hu hi on heora life gode gecwemdon,
and eac æt þam halgum þe þam hælende folgodon.

(We may take good examples,
first, from the holy patriarchs,
how they in their lives pleased God,
and also from the Saints who followed the Savior.)

(*LS* XVI.9–12)

There follows a list of holy men—patriarchs, prophets, etc.—from the Old Testament, from Abel and Enoch through Noah and Abraham down to David, Elias, and Daniel. No attempt is made to tell of their lives, but each receives a brief, lyrical comment. So of David Ælfric writes,

Dauid for his man-wyrnysse and mild-heortnysse
wearð gode gecweme and to cynincge gecoren,
swa þæt god sylf cwæð þus be him,
"Ic afunde me dauid, iessan sunu, æfter minre heortan,
seðe minne willan mid weorcum gefremð."

(David for his meekness and mildheartedness
was pleasing to God and was chosen king,
so that God Himself spoke thus concerning him,
"I have found David, Jesse's son, after my own heart,
who shall perform my will by his works.")

(*LS* XVI.55–59)

The apex of this sequence is, of course, the life of Christ Himself, which Ælfric summarizes in eighty-two lines, emphasizing the piety and devotion of those men who followed Him, the apostles and disciples. The first half of the sermon is then brought to an end with a survey of the major groups of saints who have lived since Christ, during the age of the dissemination of the faith. There are the holy martyrs,

swa micclum onbryrde
þæt hi sweltan woldon ærðan þe hi wiðsocon gode,
and heora lif aleton ærðan þe heora geleafan,
and wurdon ofslagene for ðam soðan geleafan.

(so greatly inspired
that they chose rather to die than to deny God,
and laid down their lives rather than their faith,
and were slain for the true faith.) (*LS* XVI.191–94)

Others, too:

Þa wæron halige bisceopas gehealtsume on þeawum,
and wise mæssepreostas þe wunodon on clænnysse,
and manega munecas on mycelre drohtnunge,
and clæne mædenu þe criste þeowodon
on gastlicre drohtnunge, for heora drihtnes lufan.

(Then were holy bishops, frugal in their manners,
and wise mass-priests who lived in chastity,
and many monks of excellent conduct,
and pure maidens who served Christ
in spiritual service, for their Lord's love.)

(*LS* XVI.212–16)

The classifications clearly correspond to those of the saints' lives in the series itself and suggest the comprehensive historical sweep of the saints' lives Ælfric selected.

Enumeration is the main structural device of the second half of the sermon, also. Here Ælfric turns to the virtues we can learn from the saints and the vices which they teach us to avoid. We live, he says, in the latter days of the world and the devil is especially eager to snare us,

forðan þe he wat geare þæt þysre worulde geendung
is swylce gehende, and he on-et forði.

(because he knows well that this world's ending is
very nigh at hand, and therefore he makes haste.)

(*LS* XVI.226–27)

The "three chief virtues" are, of course, faith, hope, and charity. The "eight chief sins" are gluttony, fornication, avarice, anger, sorrow, sloth, vain boasting, and pride. These are countered by the "eight chief virtues": temperance, purity, liberality, patience, spiritual joy, perseverence, love of God, and humility. The sermon ends with a call to the congregation to fight against the sins with the virtues, as did the saints, to their glory.

"The Memory of the Saints," considered as an introduction to the *Lives of Saints,* provides guidance in several ways to reading the series. Most obviously, it establishes the categories of saints which are to be followed in the collection. The lives are arranged, of course, according to the calendar of feasts, not by "categories"; but Ælfric picked and chose among the possible saints, and a general desire to offer a more or less representative selection of the types seems to underlie his particular choices.

Second, the sermon makes clear the relationship of this book of hagiographical readings to the two preceding volumes of sermons. Ælfric's general framework remains the Augustinian view of history: that human history has been guided by the power of God and that it turns around the three key events of the Fall, the Incarnation, and the Last Judgment. The Old Testament saints, Christ and His apostles, and the martyrs and confessors of the period since the Crucifixion epitomize in their lives the travails of the pious in these three ages. The *Lives of Saints* are thus as firmly grounded on the Christian view of universal history as are the *Catholic Homilies.*

Finally, the yoking in the sermon of biography and direct moralizing—the successive listings of saints and of their vices and virtues—suggests the spirit in which we should read the individual lives. The modern reader is tempted to read medieval saints' lives as crude and undeveloped biography. Often tacitly committed to evolutionary theories of literary history and preferring the realistic modes, he is likely to see the medieval saints' lives as somehow "culminating" in, say, William Roper's *Life of More,* which is comparatively "modern" in its use of historical and biographical fact. There is, of course, some truth in such a view, but it illuminates modern biography more than it does the saint's life. Ælfric and his predecessors and contemporaries did not conceive of the saint's life as bound by the same standards of historical accuracy to which they often showed themselves to be sensitive in other works. (We may compare, for example, Bede's use of the miraculous in the hagiographic and the non-hagiographic portions of the *Ecclesiastical History*.)

The saint's life was a highly conventionalized, thoroughly didactic form: as Rosemary Woolf has noted, it is "part panegyric, part epic, part romance, part sermon."[10] Its concern was less with historical fact than with spiritual truth, and its often sensational or garish action was designed to reveal a truth usually masked by the confused surface of ordinary life. The intent is not to defend the saint's life as a major literary form; for, to quote Miss Woolf again, "Though so important, the saint's life was extremely limited by its conventions. There was in it by definition a combination of simplicity and artificiality which precluded it from transcending the bounds of minor forms of literature."[11] Nevertheless, if we are to read saints' lives at all, we should approach them as highly conventionalized, didactic pieces, not as crude attempts at realistic biography.

Clearly, the second half of "The Memory of the Saints" specifies the virtues which Ælfric aims to inculcate through his *Lives* and the vices personified by the saints' antagonists. The virgin martyrs teach us purity; the confessors teach us humility and the love of God; and such saints as Chrysanthus, liberality and spiritual joy. It would, of course, be going too far to make one-to-one correlations between the individual saints and the virtues listed in the sermon; but the virtues are never far from Ælfric's mind, and he sometimes changes the tenor of a source to point a particular lesson, as when he makes St. Edmund, the martyr king, an exemplar not of chastity, but of the liberality, humility, and love of God of the Christian king. In several ways, then, "The Memory of the Saints" is a fitting and illuminating introduction to the *Lives of Saints*.

III *The Passions of Martyrs*

The saints of the Old Testament appear in the *Lives of Saints* primarily in the Bible translations—the Book of Kings (XVIII) and the Maccabees (XXV)—and may most conveniently be considered elsewhere. The next group of saints in the chronological sequence of "The Memory of the Saints" is the martyrs. A highly conventionalized pattern existed for the "passion," or account of the circumstances leading to a martyr's death.[12] Well over half of the hagiographic items in the *Lives of Saints* are passions and follow the conventional form in varying degrees. There are a number of passions of well-known Roman martyrs—St. Julian (IV), St. Sebastian (V), the Forty Soldiers (XI), and several others—and some of the lives of other saints, such as St. Edmund (XXXII), draw upon the conventions of the passion also.

The world presented by the typical passion is a highly stylized one. Although the setting is historical, it is distorted and simplified in order to magnify the hero and to emphasize the theme of perseverance and devotion. The passion often begins with an account of the saint's good works, and it often includes the circumstances of his conversion. The conflict is introduced by describing a persecution of Christians being carried out by a wicked emperor and by an equally wicked local governor. Eventually the saint is arrested and brought to a confrontation with his persecutors. One convention for the development of this section is a formal, theological debate between the saint and his judge; another is a "contest" of miracles arranged between the saint and the pagan priests. The saint, of course, remains steadfast, refusing to recant; and he is imprisoned. Conventionally, his courageous deportment in prison leads to conversions among his fellow prisoners and even among his jailers. A lengthy description of tortures and sufferings usually follows, for the persecutors attempt to break the saint's will. Often this section is handled quite sensationally; considerable ingenuity is used in devising elaborate and sometimes grotesque tortures. Finally, the saint is killed, often by beheading; his body is disposed of and sometimes an account of his posthumous miracles ends the passion.

The possibilities for extravagance in this form are obvious, and many passions, particularly the later ones, become exaggerated and grotesque. The villainy of the persecutors and the piety of the saint, the savagery of the tortures and the superhuman endurance of the saint pass all reasonable bounds. Ælfric accepts the conventions of the form; he makes no attempt to rationalize the miracles or to soften the sharp distinctions between good and evil in the narratives. But, as Dorothy Bethurum has pointed out,[13] his adaptations are notable for their restraint in handling the more lurid elements in the passions. For one thing, he avoids translating some of the more harrowing passions, though among them were some of the ones best known in Anglo-Saxon England, judging from the Old English martyrology.[14] In those Ælfric did select, he often omitted gruesome or merely sadistic passages, such as several in the life of St. Sebastian (sections IV and V) and in the life of St. Eugenia (section XIII).

In the handling of specific conventions, Ælfric, in general, follows the tradition; but his critical temperament leads to alterations here and there. His persecuting emperors—Diocletian, Claudius, Decius, Domitian—are wholly evil; he uses a few stock phrases over and over to describe them: "the wicked tormenter" ("St. Julian," IV. 104) and "the devil's worshipper" ("St. Sebastian," V. 10). The piety of the saint is equally absolute, as manifested not only by his miracles and his mass conversions. The passions of St. Julian and of the Forty Soldiers are particularly full of miracles. Among other wonders, Julian heals a blind man (IV.149 ff.) and restores a dead man to life (IV.268 ff.). Stones thrown at the Forty Soldiers miraculously turn back against the throwers (XI.100 ff.), and a frozen lake upon which they are exposed miraculously thaws (XI.95 ff.).

Most of the miracle stories which Ælfric includes from his sources are the types most common in medieval hagiography—miracles of healing, miraculous preservations from harm, and such miraculous signs of blessedness as heavenly lights and sweet odors.[15] In only three of his passions does he use the miraculous as a "test" in the conventional motif of the contest between the saint and a pagan priest. St. Julian engages in a healing contest with idol worshippers to heal a blind man (IV.149 ff.), Sebastian miraculously discovers a concealed astrological device (V.250 ff.), and St. George drinks poison safely in a contest with the sorcerer Athanasius (XIV.67 ff.).

Ælfric is similarly restrained in his use of the conventional debate between the saint and his judge, apparently to avoid boring his audience. These wholly unbelievable and often dryly theological exchanges sometimes ran to great length in early passions. Ælfric includes such passages rarely and, when he does, he often cuts them short. In "St. Julian," for example, Martianus engages in a long debate with the saint over the relative merits of the Christian and pagan gods. Ælfric abbreviates it with the words,

Þeos race is swiðe lang-sum fullice to gereccenne,
ac we hit sæcgað eow on þa scortostan wisan.

(This story is very tedious, to tell it all,
but we tell it to you in the briefest way.) (*LS* IV.139–40)

He has different compunctions about the conventional descriptions of tortures and death; here the danger is not of boring the audience but of allowing such gruesome scenes to usurp the main emphasis of the narrative. So again Ælfric abbreviates many passages and, for the most part, sticks to the more stylized and conventional torments: torture on the rack, starvation, beating, etc. An exception is the passion of St. Chrysanthus (XXXV); he is, among other torments, drenched in "ealdum miggan" (old urine) and sewed in an ox hide and placed in the sun (XXXV.158 ff.). But such grotesqueries are rare in Ælfric.

A sharp division occurs between the earlier passions and the later, more conventionalized ones, in their treatment of torture. In the earlier lives the saint feels pain and endures it through his devout perseverance. In the later lives, as the torments become more exaggerated, the convention is for the saint to be miraculously preserved from pain; and he endures in comfort the most horrendous tortures. There is, of course, a fundamental illogic here. If the saint is immune to pain, his achievement of martyrdom becomes less praiseworthy, though such immunity may testify to his general blessedness. There is also an implicit suggestion in such narratives that the blessed do not suffer in this world. This doubtless unintentional implication is clearly false, as even the example of Christ on the cross testifies.

Ælfric for the most part follows his sources in having his martyrs immune from pain. When St. George, for example, is put into a cauldron of boiling lead,

þæt lead wearð acolod þurh godes mihte
and georius sæt gesund on ðam hwere.

(the lead was cooled through God's might
and George sat sound in the cauldron.) (*LS* XIV.115–16)

A noteworthy exception, however, to this general practice is in the life of St. Vincent (XXXVII), in which perhaps the most graphic and sadistic descriptions of tortures occur. Vincent is starved, put on the rack, beaten with rods, burned with torches and hot irons, and put in a prison cell full of sharp, broken tiles. His sufferings are somewhat tempered by God's grace—angels minister to him in the prison—but he does suffer pain and eventually dies of his wounds. (In most passions, beheading is the only way the persecutors can kill the saints.)

A subtype of the martyr's passion is that which deals with the suffering and death of virgins. As we would expect from Ælfric's general interest in the theme of chastity, a number of passions of this type appear in the *Lives of Saints*: St. Eugenia (II), St. Agnes (VII), St. Agatha (VIII), St. Lucy (IX), and St. Cecilia (XXXIV). The story of St. Æthelthryth (XX), the story of Felicula in "The Chair of St. Peter" (X), and the stories of Basilissa and Daria, the chaste wives of St. Julian and St. Chrysanthus (IV and XXXV) also draw upon the conventions of this type.

One such convention appears in lives of women saints who are persecuted, suffer, and die in much the fashion of other martyrs, but who are also distinguished in the days before their martyrdom for their chastity. In such stories, a wedding-night scene often appears in which the bride and groom decline to consummate the marriage and pledge themselves to perpetual chastity. Thus St. Cecilia (XXXIV) converts her husband Valerian, and thus St. Julian (IV) converts his wife Basilissa. A similar scene appears in "The Passion of Chrysanthus and Daria" (XXXV), in which Chrysanthus converts Daria, who had been sent to seduce him; and, though they are afterward married, they live celibate lives. In the other major kind of virgin-martyr passion, the martyr is brought to grief through refusing the suit of a wooer. Thus St. Agatha (VII) refuses the attentions of the son of Sempronius, the prefect, and indignantly declares that she is wedded to Christ. When she also refuses to sacrifice to Vesta, she is placed in a house of harlots, where her virginity is miraculously preserved; but she is also finally tortured and beheaded. A number of these conventions appear in perhaps the most romantic of the virgin-martyr stories, the life of St. Eugenia (II). Eugenia disguises herself as a man and, in this disguise, eventually becomes the abbot of a monastery. Accused of attempting to seduce a wealthy widow, Eugenia clears her name by dramatically baring her breast in the courtroom.

The martyr's passion in the early Middle Ages was a form alien to modern sensibilities. It was part history, part sermon, and part fairy-tale; and modern readers are tempted to reject it as an unpalatable hybrid and as interesting only as a precursor of serious, factual history or of the romances of the High Middle Ages. To Ælfric, however, its stylized world of pagan persecution and

Christian triumph was a means of representing the permanent conflicts that underlie the confusion and chaos of ordinary life. In his versions of these popular pieces, he worked within the conventions of the form; but he also tempered their potential extravagancies with taste and reverence.

IV *The Lives of Confessors*

The earliest-acknowledged, non-biblical saints were, of course, the martyrs. But, as Christianity triumphed in Western Europe and the persecutions ceased, another group came to be recognized as saintly. These were the "confessors," men and women whose sanctity was manifested not by martyrdom but by lives of great piety and service to God, usually, though not necessarily, within the church:

> *halige bisceopas, gehealtsume on þeawum, and wise mæsse-preostas þe wunodon on clænnysse, and manega munecas on mycelre drohtnunge, and clæne mædenu þe criste þeowodon on gastlicre drohtnunge for geora drihtnes lufan.*
>
> *(holy bishops, frugal in their manners, and wise mass-priests who lived in chastity, and many monks of excellent conduct, and pure maidens who served Christ in spiritual service, for their Lord's love.)*
>
> (*LS* XVI.212–16)

The form of the confessor's life came to be as rigidly conventionalized as that of the martyr's passion.[16] Many of the conventions of the form were established and disseminated by a small group of hagiographic works which were widely known and imitated throughout Europe. Perhaps the most important of these was the *Life of St. Antony* by St. Athanasius, as translated from Greek into Latin by Bishop Evagrius of Antioch in the late fourth century; but other influential models for the confessor's life were Jerome's *Life of Paul the Hermit*, Sulpicius Severus's *Life of St. Martin*, and the *Dialogues* of Pope Gregory the Great. The form of the *Life of St. Antony* was so widely imitated that we can speak of certain conventions that pervade European hagiography as "Antonian." Some of these conventions are: (1) a prologue, in which the author professes to write at the urgent request of others and declares that he writes on good authority, either as an eyewitness or as one who has spoken to eyewitnesses; (2) an initial description of the saint's early days, including early miraculous signs of special sanctity and the circumstances of his religious vocation; (3) an account of the saint's mature career, either as a hermit, struggling against the forces of evil in isolation, or as a holy cleric; (4) a description of the heights of the saint's blessedness, often including the powers of prophecy and of healing and sometimes a sermon from the saint; (5) an account of a divine warning of death, a farewell address to disciples, and a blissful death; and, finally, (6) an account of posthumous miracles around the saint's grave or shrine. There were also conventional elements which appeared over and over in various sections of this narrative pattern: conventional statements in the prologue, conventional miracles such as lights from heaven, sweet odors around the saint, and the like, and conventional motifs for the presentation of the saint's death.

St. Antony was, of course, a hermit, whose blessedness was achieved in isolation. But the pattern of the *Life of St. Antony* could also be adapted to the life of a holy churchman. The vocation of the hermit was not to go into the desert but into the church, and the sanctity of the saint's middle life was achieved not in lonely struggles against devils but in the active life of a churchman. Thus the Antonian life could furnish a model for almost any kind of saint's life, and its simple chronological skeleton could be fleshed out with a selection of the conventional details most appropriate to the subject. Many of Ælfric's sources were modeled on the *Life of Antony*, and he preserves in his adaptations not only the basic structure but also a great many of the stock elements which functioned as Antonian conventions. He usually compresses and abbreviates the form, however, since he is usually adapting longer works into homiletic pieces.

One of the fullest and best of Ælfric's lives of confessors and one which demonstrates the Antonian pattern very clearly is the life of St. Basilius (III). St. Basil the Great (329–379) was bishop of Caesarea; Ælfric's homily for January 1, the day of his death, is based on an anonymous Latin life of the saint.[17] Like all Antonian lives, the life of Basil is arranged roughly in three parts: his early life and vocation, the sanctity of the saint's mature life, and the circumstances of his death. Basil, as a youth, studies pagan philosophy in Athens under Eubolus, the philosopher, along with

Julian, later to become emperor, and Gregory, later to become bishop. God leads Basil to turn to Christian learning, and he converts his old teacher, the two going together to be baptized in the Jordan. At his baptism, fire descends from heaven, and the Holy Spirit appears as a dove from the fire.

Basil is consecrated bishop in Caesarea; and, in response to his prayer for guidance, Christ and His apostles appear in his church to bless him. The middle section of the life, then, is dedicated to a lengthy enumeration of Basil's miracles and good works, from writing the Greek liturgy to performing miracles of healing. Many of the other miracles in this section are uncharacteristically romantic for Ælfric, who tended to minimize miracles outside the conventional types established by scriptural and early hagiographic precedent. We have a lengthy account, for example, of a young man who, Faust-like, sells his soul to the devil in return for the love of a beautiful maiden. He confesses his sin to Basil, who contends with a devil and regains the contract, telling the youth,

Ne hoga þu embe þæt;
ure hælend is swiþe wel-wyllende, and wyle þe eft under-fon,
gif þu mid soðre dædbote gecyrst eft to him.

(Do not be anxious about that;
our Saviour is very gracious, and will receive you again,
if you with true repentance will turn again to Him.)

(*LS* III.416–18)

The concluding section of the homily, which deals with the saint's last illness and death, is very full and detailed and accounts for the last hundred lines or so of the 670-line homily. When Basil is warned by a pagan leech, Joseph, that he will die shortly, Basil, eager to convert the leech, gets him to say that Basil cannot possibly live through the day. He then prays that he may live until noon of the next day. He does, and the leech is converted with all his household. Miraculously, too, a woman who had written her sins on a piece of paper finds them blotted out through Basil's deathbed prayers.

The great virtue of the St. Basil life is that Ælfric, without departing from his source, is able to present a selection from it that gives a vivid sense of his subject's character. Basil's learning and wit are clear in the homily, and even the miracle stories, though unusually extravagant, present a consistent portrait of a vigorous man contending with his intellect against a predominantly pagan society in the early days of Christianity. His adversaries can be virtuous, though pagan—as are Eubolus and Joseph—and he converts them, as Ælfric remarks, through his great learning (III. 666).

The life of St. Maur (VI) follows the same pattern, but it is only about half as long as the life of Basil. Based on a Latin life by Faustus (acknowledged by Ælfric, 1. 366), it tells the story of the holy abbot of the Franks. More ambitious in scope is the life of St. Martin (XXXI), another version of whose life Ælfric had included in the *Catholic Homilies* II (XXXIX). Both pieces are based primarily on the widely known life by Sulpicius Severus, but the second treatment in the *Lives of Saints* is over twice as long as the first, running to 1495 lines, about the length of Sulpicius's original. St. Martin was bishop of Tours from 371 to 397, the year of his death; Sulpicius was his contemporary and wrote from personal knowledge of him.

The existence of two adaptations by Ælfric of the same substantial works allows us an interesting glance into Ælfric's methods in making his adaptations.[18] In neither version does he stick to his main source; he interweaves with it other material concerning Martin drawn from Sulpicius's *Letters* and his *Dialogues* and from the *Historia Francorum* of Gregory of Tours. Ælfric's critical temperament and his conscientiousness are clear from the way he knits together material from all his sources into a clear narrative.

Ælfric's second version of the *Life of Martin* was probably not written specifically for the *Lives of Saints*, but was perhaps included to fill out the volume. Far longer than most of the *Lives*, this life is divided into fifty-five brief chapters in the manuscript. Too, although the *Lives of Saints* was probably intended for private reading, most of the items could be more easily adapted to homiletic use than could the long *Life of Martin*. Ælfric's expansions consist mainly of additional material from Sulpicius, dropped in the shorter version, and of new material concerning Martin's death from Gregory of Tours's *De virtutibus S. Martini,* a book he had probably encountered after writing the first version.

V *The English Saints*

It is not surprising that Ælfric took particular care to include several English saints in the *Lives*. Nationalistic feeling aside, the *Lives*, as a grand survey of Christian history told through the lives of its saints, would not be complete unless it were shown that God's power and grace continued to inspire men and women to saintly deeds in Ælfric's age and place. Five items, therefore, consist of lives of English saints: St. Alban, the British proto-martyr (XIX); St. Æthelthryth, the virgin queen (XX); St. Swithun, the saint of Ælfric's own Winchester (XXI); and SS. Oswald and Edmund, martyr-kings (XXVI and XXXII). These lives have always been of particular interest to readers of Ælfric and include the most frequently anthologized pieces. That they were also especially interesting to Ælfric is evident not only from the care he devoted to them but also from an eloquent passage at the end of the life of Edmund:

> *Nis angel-cynn bedæled drihtnes halgena,*
> *þonne on engla-landa licgaþ swilce halgan*
> *swylce þæs halga cyning is, and cuþberht se eadiga,*
> *and sancte æþeldryð on elig, and eac hire swustor,*
> *ansunde on lichaman, geleafan to trymminge.*
>
> *(The English nation is not deprived of the Lord's saints,*
> *since in English land lie such saints*
> *as this holy king, and the blessed Cuthbert,*
> *and Saint Æthelthryth in Ely, and also her sister,*
> *incorrupt in body, for the confirmation of the faith.)*
>
> (*LS* XXXII.259–63)

Ælfric drew heavily upon Bede for his material on native saints. Three of the lives—those of Alban, Æthelthryth, and Oswald—are adapted from Bede's *Ecclesiastical History*. The lives of Swithun and Edmund are based on Latin lives of those saints by Lantfred, "the foreigner," and by Abbo of Fleury.[19] The life of Swithun is of particular interest because Ælfric adds to Lantfred's account some of his own memories of the veneration of Swithun at Winchester. Swithun, who was bishop of Winchester, died in 862, and in the century after his death a vigorous cult had sprung up around his relics. Little was known of his life. Lantfred's work covers merely the *Translatio et Miracula S. Swithuni*, and Ælfric remarks reproachfully on the carelessness of his contemporaries who failed to record the facts of his life:

Þæt wæs þæra gymeleast þe on life hine cuþon
þæt hi noldon awritan his weorc and drohtnunge
þam towerdum mannum ðe his mihte ne cuðon.

(Such was their carelessness who knew him in life
that they would not write down his works and conversation
for future generations who did not know his power.)

(*LS* XXI.9–11)

Ælfric's account, then, consists of a description of how Swithun appeared some years after his death to a faithful smith (1. 24) to tell him to carry word to the authorities that he desired that his body be exhumed and moved into the new church of St. Peter. After several miracles had testified to the validity of this vision, the body was moved; the rest of the work consists of an enumeration of the ensuing miracles, mostly miracles of healing. One miracle related to Ælfric's personal experience is the appearance of Swithun in a vision to reproach the monks who had become careless in performing their duty to sing the Te Deum each time a healing occurred. The monks corrected their error, and Ælfric remembers,

Hi hit heoldon þa syððan symle on ge-wunon,
swa swa we gesawon sylfe for oft,
and þone sang we sungon unseldon mid heom.

(From then on they always observed this custom,
as we ourselves have very often seen,
and have not seldom sung this hymn with them.)

(*LS* XXI.262–64)

Ælfric is also apparently writing from his personal memories of Winchester near the end of the life when he describes (11. 432 ff.) how the walls of the church at Winchester were hung full of the crutches and stools of cripples who had been healed by Swithun. The last lines of the life are also notable for the mixture of nostalgia and bitterness when Ælfric, writing in the dark days of Æthelred's reign and the Danish assaults, recalls the peace and order of the days of his youth:

We habbað nu gesæd be swiðune þus sceortlice,
and we secgað to soðan þæt se tima wæs gesælig
and wynsum on angel-cynne, þaða eadgar cynincg
þone cristen-dom ge-fyrðrode, and fela munuclifa arærde,
and his cynerice wæs wunigende on sibbe,
swa þæt man ne gehyrde gif ænig scyp-here wære,
buton agenre leode þe ðis land heoldon.

(We have now spoken thus briefly of Swithun,
and we say of a truth that the time was blessed
and winsome in England, when King Edgar
furthered Christianity, and built many monasteries,
and his kingdom still continued in peace,
so that no fleet was heard of,
save that of the people themselves who held this land.)

(*LS* XXI.434–49)

The most elaborate of the lives of English saints, and in some ways the finest achievement of Ælfric's work in the saint's-life form, is the life of King Edmund (XXXII). King Edmund was a fairly obscure East Anglian king who was killed by the Danes in 870. In the century after his death, a cult sprang up around his burial place; and, in time, his legend came to be one of the most extensive bodies of English hagiographic material; for it gathered accretions from folk tale and eventually assumed the character of medieval romance.[20] Ælfric added little to the legend as it came to him through the *Passio Sancti Eadmundi* of Abbo of Fleury, but his treatment of the material is notable for the way he subtly reinterprets the character of Edmund by drawing upon both hagiographic conventions and those of Germanic epic. The result is a brief, but effective "Christian epic" in which the ideals of heroic pagan society and those of Christianity merge.

Abbo professed to write from a source directly connected to Edmund's death. Edmund's sword-bearer, who witnessed the martyrdom, was said to have described it to Archbishop Dunstan when Dunstan was a young man at the court of King Æthelstan; Dunstan, just before his death, passed the story on to Abbo; and it was thus transmitted orally across a hundred years or so by only three informants. Ælfric, who begins his account by summarizing these facts in ordinary prose, changes to his heightened poetic-prose style for the legend itself. Edmund ruled over the East Angles until the Danes landed under the command of Hingwar and Hubba.

After ravaging the land, the Danes arrive in East Anglia and send Edmund a threatening message, demanding that he surrender. Edmund, who sends back a brave and eloquent reply, refuses either to submit or flee; he will receive the Danes without weapons as Christ would have done (11. 103–04). The Danes seize him, tie him to a tree, shoot him full of arrows, and then behead him. When the Danes have departed and when Edmund's people seek his body, they find his head guarded by a great gray wolf and miraculously calling to guide the searchers. They bury the head and body and raise a church on the spot, where many miracles are performed.

Ælfric follows Abbo very closely in the outlines of this simple tale; his major change is that he greatly compresses the story, making his version less than half as long as Abbo's. But, in the process of compression, he changes the whole tone and spirit of the legend. Abbo makes Edmund a wholly unbelievable stereotype who rather complacently seeks martyrdom knowing he will be rewarded in Heaven. His reply to the Danes is in highly ornate Latin prose and is heavily theological in content. Ælfric takes particular care in recasting the whole exchange between Edmund and the Danes. Behind Edmund's simple and forthright reply lies the whole tradition of Germanic epic heroism, one strangely transmuted by the spirit of Christian charity:

Þæs ic gewilnige and gewisce mid mode,
þæt ic ana ne belife æfter minum leofum þegnum,
þe on heora bedde wurdon mid bearnum, and wifum,
færlice ofslægene fram þysum flot-mannum.
Næs me næfre gewunelic þæt ic worhte fleames,
ac ic wolde swiðor sweltan, gif ic þorfte,
for minum agenum earde; and se ælmihtiga god wat
þæt ic nelle abugan fram his biggengum æfre,
ne fram his soþan lufe, swelte ic lybbe ic.

(This I desire and wish in my mind,
that I should not be left alone after my dear thanes,
who in their beds, with children and wives,
have suddenly been slain by these seamen.
It was never my way to take to flight,
but I would rather die, if I must,
for my own land; and the almighty God knows
that I will never turn aside from His worship,
nor from His true love, whether I die or live.) (*LS* XXXII.74–82)

Ælfric presents Edmund as a heroic Christian king, the product of the English blending of the traditions of kingship inherited from pagan Germanic culture on one side and Christian doctrine on the other. The warrior-kings of the Germanic tribes were first among equals; they wielded their weapons alongside their men, seeking fame in battle and accepting the obligation of giving protection to those who served them. To the Christian, the kingly office came to be equated with the priesthood; the king was God's vicar, and he took oaths not only to his people but to God Himself. The coronation of King Edgar, which took place late in his reign—delayed probably until Edgar had reached the canonical age for ordination to the priesthood—was presided over by Archbishop Dunstan. Edgar's prayers and oaths, his anointing, and the ecclesiastical flavor of the whole ceremony indicated that he was a king who ruled "by the grace of God." A similar synthesis underlies Ælfric's characterization of King Edmund—king and martyr.

Much of what we have said in Chapter 3 about Ælfric's achievement as a homilist may also be applied to his work as a hagiographer. In the *Lives of Saints*, as in the *Catholic Homilies*, his selection of material, his interpretations, and his doctrine are highly orthodox; his style is lucid and eloquent; and his attitude toward his audience is sensitive and sympathetic without being condescending. Taken individually, a number of the lives—those of St. Basilius, St. Martin, and St. Edmund, for example—are among the high points of Old English prose. Considered as a whole, the individual parts of the *Lives of Saints* are unified by the large design indicated in the introductory "Memory of the Saints." And, considered as part of the general educational plan that underlies all Ælfric's literary work, the *Lives* occupies a place very near the center of that plan.

Reading the *Lives* in the twentieth century, we are continually tempted to emphasize elements in them which were probably peripheral to Ælfric's major purposes. The saints' lives are only incidentally precursors of realistic biography, revelations of Old English life, reminiscences of epic, or anticipations of romance. Their central purpose, as Ælfric suggests in "The Memory of the Saints," was identical to that of the *Catholic Homilies*: to reveal the spiritual truth of the great divine pattern that underlay the bewildering variety of historical fact. But, whereas the *Catholic Homilies* had dealt directly with the power of God as it moves through human history, *Lives of Saints* deals with that power as it had been revealed in the long series of holy men from the Old Testament saints through Christ and His apostles, the martyrs of the early Christian era, and the confessors of more recent times. If we have lost this perspective, we may value the *Lives* for the eloquence of their prose, for the vigor of their narrative style, for the charm of their stylized portraiture; but we should remember that they draw their life from the high purpose which inspired them.

CHAPTER 4

Bible Translations

ACCOUNTS of the history of the translation of the Bible into English generally credit Ælfric with being the first important translator. If this claim is to be substantiated, a rather broad interpretation of "translation" must be adopted. As we have seen, a number of Ælfric's homilies are scriptural and the summaries of several biblical books appear in his collections; but these are hardly translations in the ordinary sense. Perhaps his closest approach to strict translation is his version of the first part of Genesis, which appears in the so-called *Old English Heptateuch;* and he undertook even this work with strong misgivings, which he expressed in the preface to Genesis.

He had expressed similar misgivings much earlier, of course, about treating holy matters in the native tongue and thus running the risk of exposing them to the contempt of the ignorant and vicious. In an epilogue to the second series of *Catholic Homilies,* he had written,

Ic cweðe nu þæt ic næfre heononforð ne awende godspel oþþe godspeltrahtas of Ledene on Englisc.

(I say now that henceforth I will never turn gospel or gospel-exposition from Latin into English.) (*CH* II, 594)

Again, in the Latin preface to the *Lives of Saints*, he expressed qualms about writing homilies in English:

I do not promise, however, to write very many in this tongue, because it is not fitting that many should be translated into our language, lest peradventure the pearls of Christ be had in disrespect. (*LS*, Latin Preface, 3)

And at the end of the preface to Genesis, written about 997, he wrote,

Ic cweðe nu ðæt ic ne dearr ne ic nelle nane boc æfter ðisre of Ledene on Englisc awendan.

(I say now that I neither dare to nor will translate any book hereafter from Latin into English.) (Crawford, 80)

Ælfric apparently overcame, to some degree, his reservations about translating Holy Writ later in life, for in the *Letter to Sigeweard* he expresses no doubts about the propriety of translating the books he mentions. Nevertheless, he remains something of a biblical translator *malgré lui*.

A survey of Ælfric's biblical translations should begin with the numerous, though scattered, passages of Scripture which appear in the homilies. The *lectiones*, plus the scriptural passages which appear in the bodies of the homilies, amount to a considerable body of work; and separate consideration might be given to *Catholic Homilies* II.XXXV, which is a homiletic epitome of the Book of Job. A second category of biblical pieces is the summaries of Old Testament books: Kings, the Maccabees, Judges, Esther, and Judith. Peter Clemoes has suggested a rationale for these summaries in relation to Ælfric's general plan. Ælfric had expounded much of the typology of the significant events of the Old Testament in the *Catholic Homilies*. He had also drawn upon the Old Testament for moral exempla, but had not treated it systematically on the level of moral interpretation. "And so, as an appendix to his homilies, he provided summary narratives of certain Old Testament books, narratives that with very little elucidation made the point that obedience to God is best."[1] Kings and the Maccabees were included in the *Lives of Saints* (XVIII and XXV). The others which followed—Judges, Esther, and Judith—suggested particular moral lessons, as Ælfric explained in the *Letter to Sigeweard*.

Ælfric's contribution to the so-called *Old English Heptateuch* completes his work in biblical translation. This editorial compilation of Old English translations of the first seven books of the Bible was formerly assigned principally to Ælfric, but it now appears certain that the only Ælfrician translations which appear in it are the first part of Genesis, the last part of Numbers, Joshua, and the version of Judges mentioned above.

I *Old English Bible Translation before Ælfric*

Ælfric's varied pieces of Bible translation amount to a larger body of work than any other Old English Bible translations; nevertheless, some tradition of Bible translation did exist when he began his work,[2] although the first steps in the direction of an English version of the Bible had been taken rather slowly. There is no mention of any attempts in this direction during the first century after Christianity was introduced into England in 597. The work of Cædmon, the unlettered Whitby cowherd whose story is told by Bede, and the "Cædmonian" Old English poems on Genesis, Exodus, Daniel, and Judith can hardly be called translations; but such "Christian epics" seem to have taken the place of any attempt to produce a native version of the Bible until the tenth century.

There was a long-standing tradition that Bede had translated large portions of the Bible into English, but the only contemporary evidence of this is the passage in Cuthbert's *Life of Bede* in which he describes how Bede dictated the final words of a translation of the Gospel of St. John with his dying breath. If there ever was such a translation, it has perished, along with any other Bible translations Bede may have made. Other traditions, similarly doubtful, credit Aldhelm, the seventh-century abbot of Malmesbury, with a translation of at least the Psalms and perhaps even more, and King Alfred with extensive translating projects.

Such legends aside, the surviving texts which, along with the Cædmonian poems, anticipate Ælfric are mostly glosses. Such insertions of Old English translations between the lines of a Latin text are fairly numerous. The earliest surviving example appears to be a text of the Psalms, known as the Vespasian Psalter, which dates from about 825. At least ten other glossed Psalters of later dates also survive. The Gospels were the other portion of the Bible most frequently glossed. The Lindisfarne Gospels, one of the most beautiful of Old English books, was glossed in the Northumbrian dialect about 950, and a North Mercian gloss was inserted in the Rushworth Gospels somewhat later. Although these glosses generally give an equivalent for every word in the text, they can hardly be called independent translations; for they follow the Latin word order and make no attempt to capture English idiom.

The most ambitious project, however, and one which may be called a genuine translation, was a version of the four Gospels in West Saxon about the middle of the tenth century. Four manuscripts from the eleventh century and two more from the twelfth century have been preserved of this work, testifying to some fairly widespread and continuing interest in it. These "West Saxon Gospels" are very competent translations, and they reveal a good command both of Latin and of English idiom. They are generally held to be the work of three translators, one who did Matthew, another who did Mark and Luke, and a third who did John. Arthur H. Abel, however, has recently argued that all four Gospels should be attributed to Ælfric.[3] The evidence for such an attribution, attractive as it may be, is very slight and subjective, as Abel himself admits. Whoever the author or authors might have been, the Gospels are the product of the same monastic revival of which Ælfric was a part; he probably knew them; and his own concentration upon the Old Testament may have been based upon a wish to supplement this already existing selection from the New Testament.

The work of the Old English Bible translators before Ælfric was not extensive, and the political chaos of the eleventh century was to dash any prospect that it would have culminated in a complete Old English version of the Bible. But it was notable for its high points—the Cædmonian poetic paraphrases and the West Saxon Gospels—and for its early date: England was one of the earliest of European countries to produce even this much of a vernacular Bible. Ælfric did not benefit notably from it; he wrote primarily to supply a pressing need rather than to contribute to an already existing tradition. But his forerunners did supply a precedent for his work, and perhaps we may see in the styles of the old poetic renderings and of the West Saxon Gospels general inspirations for Ælfric's rhythmic manner and his own clarity and simplicity.

II *Ælfric's Theory of Translation*

Ælfric's method of free translation—sometimes rendering fairly exactly and sometimes condensing, paraphrasing, or elaborating—is reminiscent of the famous metaphor which appears in the preface to King Alfred's translation of St. Augustine's *Soliloquies,* in which Alfred defended his own freedom of selection and arrangement:

Gaderode me þonne kigclas, and stuþansceaftas, and lohsceaftas, ond hylfa to ælcum þara tola þe ic mid wircan cuðe; and bohtimbru and bolttimbru to ælcum þara weorca þe ic wyrcan cuðe, þa wlitegostan treowo be þam dele ðe ic aberan meihte. Ne com ic naþer mid anre byrðene ham, þe me ne lyste ealne þane wude ham brengan, gif ic hyne ealne aberan meihte. On ælcum treowe ic geseah hwæthwugu þæs þe ic æt ham beþorfte. Forþam ic lære ælcne ðara þe maga si ond manigne wæn hæbbe, þæt he menige to þam ilcan wuda þar ic ðas stuðansceaftas cearf, fetige hym þar ma, and gefeðrige hys wænas mid fegrum gerdum, þat he mage windan manigne smicerne wah, and manig ænlic hus settan and fegerne tun timbrian þara, and þær murge and softe mid mæge oneardian ægðer ge wintras ge sumeras, swa swa ic nu gyt ne dyde.

(I gathered for myself staves, and stud-shafts, and cross-beams, and handles for each of the tools that I could work with; and bow-timbers and bolt-timbers for every work that I could do, as many as I could carry of the comeliest trees. Neither did I come home with a burden, for it pleased me not to bring all the wood home, even if I could bear it. In each tree I saw something that I needed at home; therefore I advise every one who is able, and who has many wagons, to direct his steps to the same wood where I cut the stud-shafts. Let him there obtain more for himself, and load his wagons with fair twigs, so that he may build many a neat wall, and many a rare house, and a fair enclosure, and live in it in joy and comfort both winter and summer, as I have not yet done.[4]

Ælfric himself commented often on his methods in the prefaces to his own translations. Almost invariably, except in the preface to Genesis, such comments appear in the Latin prefaces rather than the English ones. They thus seem to be addressed, unlike the translations themselves, to learned readers who might oppose both translation into the vernacular in general and Ælfric's methods in particular. As early as the preface to the first series of *Catholic Homilies,* Ælfric made explicit a philosophy of translation which he repeated in later prefaces and to which, despite the development of his style, he remained faithful in practice through the rest of his career. First of all, he translates sense for sense, not word for word. (A similar opposition had been expressed in the Proem to the Old English translation of Boethius's *Consolation of Philosophy.* King Alfred, the author said, had translated this work sometimes word for word; sometimes sense for sense.)[5] Second, the style is to be simple and unadorned, the better to reach the hearts of the untutored for whom the works are intended. He eschews rhetorical ornament in favor of "the pure and open words of the language of this people" (*CH* I, Latin Preface, 1).

The Latin prefaces to the *Lives of Saints* and the *Grammar* express substantially the same intentions. Ælfric repeats that his method is to translate sense for sense and that he has willingly abbreviated and epitomized in order to avoid boring his listeners. The *Grammar* is for "tender youths" and he has therefore simplified his explanations, though he knows that words may be interpreted in many ways. If Ælfric seems somewhat on the defensive concerning his methods of translation in the *Homilies* and the *Lives of Saints*, he was doubly so when he came to biblical translation. Those who opposed translation of the Fathers into the vernacular would have certainly objected to translation, especially a free one, of the Scriptures. Ælfric is likely to have known the strictures that St. Jerome had laid upon biblical translation. Jerome, translator of the Vulgate Bible, had expressed his own theory of translation most fully in his *Preface to Eusebius* and *Epistle to Pammachius*. In the *Preface to Eusebius*, he recommends strongly giving sense for sense, rather than word for word, "except in the case of the Holy Scriptures where even the order of words is a mystery."[6]

St. Jerome's comments, and the natural diffidence that Ælfric felt in attempting scriptural translation, explain why the English preface to Genesis contains a particularly full explanation and defense of his methods. The task, Ælfric says, is a dangerous one:

> Nu þincð me, leof, þæt þæt weorc is swiðe þleolic me oððe ænigum men to underbeginnenne, for þan þe ic ondræde, gif sum dysig man þas boc ræt oððe rædan gehyrþ, þæt he wille wenan, þæt he mote lybban nu on þære niwan æ, swa swa þa ealdan fæderas leofodon þa on þære tide, ær þan þe seo ealde æ gesett wære, oþþe swa swa men leofodon under Moyses æ.
>
> (Now it seems to me, sir, that this work is very dangerous for me or anyone else to undertake, for I fear that, if some foolish man should read this book or hear it read, he would think that he could live now, under the New Law, just as the Patriarchs lived in that time, before the Old Law was established, or as men lived under the law of Moses.) (Crawford, 76)

Ælfric warns the reader that he will confine himself to setting forth the bare text and will avoid interpretation:

> We secgað eac foran to þæt seo boc is swiþe deop gastlice to understandenne, and we writaþ na mare buton þa nacedan gerecednisse. Þonne þincþ þam ungelæredum þæt eall þæt andgit beo belocen on þære anfealdan gerecednisse, ac hit ys swiþe feor þam.

(I say in advance that this book has a very deep spiritual meaning, and I write no more than the naked facts. The unlearned will think that all the meaning is contained in the simple narrative, but this is far from true.) (Crawford,77)

Ælfric has clearly wrestled with Jerome's admonition that even the word order is sacred in Holy Scripture, and has attempted to reconcile it with his own conviction that a faithful translation must be true to the nature of the new language:

We ne durron na mare awritan on Englisc þonne ðæt Leden hæfð, ne ða endebyrdnysse awendan, buton ðam anum, ðæt ðæt Leden and ðæt Englisc nabbað na ane wisan on ðære spræce fadunge: æfre se ðe awent oððe se ðe tæcð of Ledene on Englisc, æfre he sceal gefadian hit swa ðæt ðæt Englisc hæbbe his agene wisan, elles hit bið swyðe gedwolsum to rædenne ðam ðe ðæs Ledenes wise ne can.

(I dare write no more in English than the Latin has, nor change the word order, except insofar as Latin and English differ in their idioms. Whoever translates or teaches from Latin into English must always arrange it so that the English is idiomatic, else it is very misleading to one who does not know the Latin idiom.) (Crawford, 79–80)

Through all Ælfric's prefaces, and especially in the English preface to Genesis, he reveals that his translation methods were the result of careful consideration and deliberate choice. Well aware that other learned men may object to his practices, he has adopted them nonetheless for particular purposes and to meet specific needs. He is, however, eager to overcome possible objections from his contemporaries and to attempt to reconcile his methods with the recommendations of patristic authority. For, in the matter of translation, as in his choice of texts and his methods of interpretation, he wants his work to express the best thought of his day and to win the approval of the faithful and learned.[7]

III *The* Letter to Sigeweard

Shortly after Ælfric became Abbot of Eynsham in 1005, he wrote a piece variously known as the *Letter to Sigeweard* and *On the Old And New Testaments*. The *Letter* is a brief, popular exposition of the Bible, original with Ælfric, though he is indebted to such works as St. Augustine's *De Doctrina Christiana.* It may usefully be considered along with Ælfric's Bible translations not only because it provides an interesting summary of his interpretations of biblical material but also because, throughout the *Letter,* Ælfric alludes to his own English versions of various books of the Bible.

Little is known of the Sigeweard to whom the *Letter* is addressed. A Sigeweard signed the Eynsham charter, and the *Letter* itself establishes that Sigeweard had entertained Ælfric at his estate and had often asked him for his books. At the end of the *Letter,* Ælfric mildly rebukes Sigeweard for having pressed him to drink more than was desirable when he visited him, and points out that "over-drinking" destroys both a man's soul and his safety. Earlier in the *Letter,* however, Ælfric specifically praises Sigeweard for his "godan weorc," and later he inserts a few words on the theme of Christ's injunction, "If ye love me, keep my commandments." Christ, Ælfric says, loves the deed more than the smooth word (Crawford, 57–58), possibly an additional allusion to Sigeweard's virtue.

The *Letter,* which surveys in order the books of the Bible, classifies them, summarizes most of them very briefly, and comments on the place of each in the scriptural canon. Ælfric seems to make a particular point of mentioning his own English treatments of biblical material in the appropriate places, possibly in response to a particular request of Sigeweard, who had asked Ælfric for his English writings (Crawford, 16). He makes thirteen such allusions, some of them very specific, as when he refers to his homily on the sevenfold gifts (Crawford, 18), and some general, as when he mentions his many homilies on the Gospels (Crawford, 56). The *Letter* is thus invaluable in the study of Ælfric's canon as well as for its reflection of Ælfric's overall view of the Bible.

Throughout the *Letter,* Ælfric emphasizes, as he repeatedly did elsewhere, the unity and coherence of sacred history. As in *De Initio Creaturae* (CH.I.I), in *De Creatore et Creatura,* and in its sequel *De Sex Aetatibus Mundi,* he stresses the pattern of Creation-Fall-Redemption-Judgment that lies behind the variety of history and of biblical literature. Thus, throughout his progression through the books of the Bible, he is careful to show how each fits into the design of God's plan, and thus, at the end of the work, he provides a retrospective view of the "six ages of the world" as another way of showing the unity of universal history.

Ælfric's brief passages of interpretation are primarily typological and moral. He reminds Sigeweard that "each holy father by words and deeds clearly gives testimony to our Savior and His coming" (Crawford, 24). He does not, of course, provide exhaustive typological interpretations of the Old Testament in his short introduction, but he does mention the most important points: Adam, created on the sixth day, prefigures Christ, whose birth began the sixth age of the world; Eve betokens the Church; Abel's murder prefigures the Crucifixion, and so on. Moral instruction is similarly brief, though pointed. Of the Book of Judges, Ælfric says,

Ic þohte þæt ge woldon þurh wundorlican race
eower mod awendan to Godes willan on eornost.

(I thought that you would, through this wonderful history,
turn your mind to God's will in earnest.) (Crawford, 34)

The books of Judith and the Maccabees are made to yield a topical moral: that the English should defend their land against foreign armies (Crawford, 48). A number of moral interpretations appear, but the major moral point which Ælfric makes in the treatise, and one to which he returns several times, is that works are more valuable than words. The *Letter* begins with a statement of this idea, an appropriate one in a work addressed to a pious but not particularly learned layman:

Ic secge þe to soðan,
þæt se bið swiþe wis, se þe mid weorcum spricð,
and se hæfð forþgang for Gode and for worulde,
se ðe mid godum weorcum hine sylfne geglengð.

(I tell you truly
that he is very wise, who speaks with works,
and he proceeds well with both God and the world,
who furnishes himself with good works.)

(Crawford, 15)

Sigeweard himself is praised for his good works, and man's justifiable pride in his good deeds is equated with God's pride in His own works. The Maccabees did not fight "with fair words only," but with "victorious deeds" (Crawford, 49). Similar observations appear throughout the *Letter,* and Ælfric ends, just before the final personal note on drinking, with this comment:

Nu miht þu wel witan, þæt weorc sprecað swiþor
þonne þa nacodan word, þe nabbað nane fremminge.
Is swa þeah god weorc on þam godan wordum,
þonne man oðerne lærð and to geleafan getrimð
mid þære soþan lare, and þonne mann wisdom sprecð
manegum to þearfe and to rihtinge, þæt God se geherod, seþe a rixað. Amen.

(Now you may well understand, that works speak more
than naked words which achieve nothing.
Yet there is good work in good words,
as when a man teaches another and leads him to faith
with true knowledge, and when a man speaks wisdom
to many for their needs and their guidance, to the praise of God,
who reigns forever. Amen. (Crawford, 74)

This distrust of "good words," qualified though it is, may appear to be a rather surprising moral lesson to derive from a summary account of Holy Scripture. But it is thoroughly in keeping with Ælfric's practical temperament and points up the nature of his own translations, summaries, and adaptations of Scripture. He is never centrally concerned with learning for its own sake, but always has a particular moral purpose in mind in producing an English version of Scripture, always strives to bring about "good work in good words."

IV *Bible Translations in the* Catholic Homilies

Ælfric translated a considerable body of biblical material while composing the *Catholic Homilies.*[8] The *lectiones* are all translated, short biblical passages are frequently cited illustratively, and certain homilies are principally concerned with the retelling of biblical narratives. A serious difficulty in studying his methods in making these translations—and his other Bible translations as well—is that we do not know the exact recension of the Latin Bible from which he worked. The textual history of the Vulgate Bible in the Middle Ages is very complicated,[9] and our knowledge of the versions current in Ælfric's day is too limited to permit any reliable observations on his translations of specific verses. All comments must be based on the assumption that he used a "standard" recension of the Vulgate—one close to the modern authorized Vulgate—and must correspondingly be taken as tentative.

Despite Ælfric's expressed sensitivity to the special responsibilities of the Bible translator, no obvious differences in method separate his Bible translations from his others. As in his translations and adaptations of the Fathers, he is constantly and perhaps centrally concerned with the needs of his audience. His changes are, therefore, of two kinds. First, he strives to simplify and clarify narrative and exposition so the work may be easily grasped when presented orally to simple, uneducated people. Second, he tries to make the moral content of the material as clear and unambiguous as possible. He sometimes adds a comment which draws an explicit moral; at other times he silently omits details which might obscure the moral lesson or which might be misunderstood by his hearers.

One way of simplifying his material was to omit anything that might seem confusing, irrelevant, or repetitious. In *Catholic Homilies* I.XXII, he translates the account of the Day of Pentecost found in the second chapter of Acts. Although he follows the order of the account fairly closely, he makes a number of small omissions, the reasons for which we can probably deduce. Verses 9–11 are largely dropped, apparently because they contain a number of unfamiliar and unnecessary proper names. Small redundancies are eliminated, as when *stupebant autem omnes,* which begins both verses 7 and 12, is rendered only once as *"ða wearð seo menigu swiðe ablicged"* (1. 60).

Sometimes omissions seem to be motivated by a general desire for conciseness and economical expression, rather than by any particular objection to the omitted material. Thus in the same homily, in translating Acts 2:14–35, he omits parts of verses 17, 19, 33, and 34, and all of verses 18 and 20 through 31; and the result, a speech of Peter's, is pointed and effective, gaining power through its relative brevity. Another kind of alteration Ælfric makes fairly freely is the rearrangement of material. Again, he seems to be motivated in these changes by a desire for clarity and consistency. In *Catholic Homilies* I.VI, on "The Octaves and Circumcision of Our Lord" (11. 16–35), he translates the passage on the covenant of circumcision from Genesis, chapter 17; and he arranges the verses quite freely to clarify the sequence of events. Verse 5 is changed to a place before verse 15 to bring together the references to God's changing the names of Abram and Sarai to Abraham and Sarah, and verse 3 is moved to follow verse 7 to divide God's speech into two clear parts, separated by Abraham's falling on his knees.

This kind of transposition and rearrangement sometimes results, as it also does in the non-biblical translations, in a new narrative constructed of details drawn from widely separated sources. In *Catholic Homilies* I.XXI, Ælfric translates the account of the Ascension from Acts 1:1–15, in which it is said that the apostles returned to Jerusalem from the Mount of Olives without any preparatory reference to their having left Jerusalem. Ælfric supplies this lack by drawing upon the parallel section in Luke, and the result is this kind of an interweaving of the two Gospels:

> And he lædde hi ða ut of ðære byrig up [from Luke 20.51]
> to anre dune ðe is gecweden mons Oliveti [from Acts 1.12],
> and hi gebletsode up-ahafenum handum [from Luke 20.50].
> þa mid þære bletsunge ferde he [from Luke 20.51].
>
> (And He led them out of the city [from Luke 20.51]
> to a hill which is called the Mount of Olives [from Acts 1.12],
> and blessed them with hands uplifted [from Luke 20.50].
> Then with the blessing he departed [from Luke 20.51].)
>
> (*CH* II.XXI, 18–20)

An even more striking composite of biblical material is Ælfric's account of the laying of Christ's body in the sepulchre and of His resurrection in *Catholic Homilies* I.XV. His principal source is Matthew, but he draws upon all three of the other Gospels as well. He translates about a third of the verses he uses exactly, alters the rest of them slightly, and provides a few short passages of transition of his own where necessary.

A final kind of change Ælfric makes in his translations of biblical material in the *Catholic Homilies* is additions of interpretative comment. Many examples of such additions could be cited; Charles R. Davis has pointed out an interesting one in *Catholic Homilies* I.III, on the Passion of St. Stephen. Ælfric's source, in Acts, does not mention that Stephen's persecutors are Jews. But Ælfric, at least four times, explicitly identifies them as Jews (11. 17, 23, 50, and 56). Conversely, Ælfric consistently adds to Stephen's name the epithets "se eadiga" (the blessed) or "se halga" (the holy) (11. 13, 30–31, 52, and 61–62). Davis concludes that "Ælfric deliberately stresses the guilt of the Jews and . . . is ever careful to preserve in his hearers the desired attitude both toward the Jews and toward his subject, Stephen."[10]

V *The Homily on Job*

The most extended rendering of the Bible in the *Catholic Homilies* is *Catholic Homilies* II.XXXV, a homiletic epitome of the Book of Job. It is difficult to decide whether to call this piece a paraphrase or a translation: the treatment is certainly very free, and yet over half the lines in the homily are very direct translations of the biblical book. Ælfric never produced a careless or mechanical translation, but few better examples can be given of his great attention to detail in reshaping a source for his intended audience.[11]

After a short preface, Ælfric begins the homily with a translation of the first eight verses of Job. These verses are very closely translated except for verses 4 and 5, where Ælfric omits a reference which might suggest that Job's sons engaged in dissipation, and another to burnt offerings. In the first case, Ælfric seemingly wishes to avoid suggesting that Job's sons, who afterward appear guiltless, were guilty of any wrongdoing; and, in the second, he seems to want to avoid reminding his hearers of pagan practices of worship. He therefore translates *holocausta* (burnt offerings) as "seofonfealde lac" (sevenfold gifts).

These eight verses are followed by a passage added by Ælfric explaining Satan's helplessness in the presence of God; for Ælfric is again anticipating his listeners' lack of sophistication and their possible confusion over Satan's being allowed to appear before God. Ælfric next inserts a translation of a series of verses from chapters 29 (verses 12–16) and 31 (verses 20, 16–17, 25, 29, and 32–42). In these verses, Job describes his own virtuous ways of life. The result is a short "character" of the ideal rich man: benevolent to the poor and the unfortunate and ever ready to confess his sins. Ælfric then continues with a translation of the rest of the first chapter, omitting only verse 13, another reference to Job's sons' eating and drinking. He concludes this first section with a brief passage of commentary, denouncing Satan and praising Job.

The second chapter is translated relatively closely, with only small and insignificant omissions. Additions and alterations are also minor: short interpretative comments after verses 6 and 10 explain why Job was tried and draw an analogy with Adam's temptation through Eve in the Garden. Interestingly, the "comforters" are described as "þry cyninges" (three kings) and "gesibbe" (kinsmen), apparently in an attempt to exalt Job even more. Ælfric's most radical compression of his source comes in the middle section, where chapters 3–41, the long poetic debate between Job and his comforters, is summarized in a few lines. This passage ends with a dramatic expression of Job's faith in God, taken from chapter 19 (verses 25–27). The homily ends with a fairly close translation of Job 42:7–16 and a brief final passage of original explanation and interpretation.

Ælfric's version of Job is not an equivalent of the biblical text, nor was it meant to be. It was intended for a particular use: oral delivery before an unsophisticated audience in need of moral instruction. Ælfric's changes serve two purposes, one narrative and one moral. He is concerned to reduce the length of the book to make it suitable for delivery as a homily and to make the narrative line so clear that it could be immediately grasped upon one hearing, even by the ignorant. He is also concerned that the moral lesson be just as clear and unambiguous to the same audience. Ælfric's Job is a simplified and idealized portrait of the virtuous rich man in good fortune and in bad. As such a portrait, the homily is eminently successful.

VI *Epitomes of Old Testament Books*

Another group of works that may be regarded as free Bible translations may be surveyed briefly as a group. These are a series of paraphrases of the Old Testament books of Kings, the Maccabees, Esther, Judith, Judges, and Joshua. As we have already mentioned, Clemoes has pointed out that these books have in common the moral lesson that "obedience to God is best." They were probably intended as an "appendix to the homilies," which had expounded the typology of the Old Testament comparatively thoroughly but had not given systematic treatment to its moral interpretation.

The paraphrases of Kings and the Maccabees appear in the *Lives of Saints* as numbers XVIII and XXV. Both are presented frankly as reading pieces; neither has a homiletic introduction and neither seems to be restricted in length by the limits of homiletic presentation. Ælfric mentions his English versions of both books in the *Letter to Sigeweard*: Kings, in lines 507–508; and the books of the Maccabees, in lines 836–38:

Ic awende hig on Englisc
and rædon gif ge wyllað eow sylfum to ræde.

(I have translated them into English;
read them if you wish for your own instruction.) (Crawford, 51)

How compressed a version of Kings Ælfric wrote may be judged by the fact that in 481 lines he covers the major episodes of both 1 and 2 Kings as well as some other material from 1 Samuel. Essentially, Ælfric has selected passages which describe the major figures in this section of the Bible and has strung them together to suggest the sequence of Hebrew kings. He begins with passages from 1 Samuel, chapters 13, 16, and 17, which describe Saul and David. He then picks up the story with Ahab, from 1 Kings, chapter 17. The life of Solomon is silently omitted, perhaps because of his spectacular marital career, about which Ælfric elsewhere expressed fears that it might mislead the unsophisticated. The last two hundred and fifty lines or so cover 2 Samuel in the biblical sequence but with many omissions.

The moral lesson of the Book of Kings is made explicit by Ælfric both in the *Letter to Sigeweard* and at the end of his paraphrase. Some of the kings were righteous, he says in the *Letter* (11. 508 ff.), while others were evil and fared very badly. At the end of the paraphrase, he is equally pointed:

se þe synnum gehyrsumað
and godes beboda forsyhð, nu þæs godspelles timan,
þæt he bið þam cynincgum gelic ðe gecuron deofolgild,
and heora scyppend forsawon.

(he who obeys sins
and despises God's commands, now in the gospel's age,
is like the kings who chose idolatry,
and despised their Creator.)

(*LS* XVIII.475–79)

The Maccabees is also radically compressed in Ælfric's summary. Passages from both books are woven together to summarize, in 811 lines, the story of the battles of Judas Maccabeus. The passages selected are translated fairly closely, but Ælfric knits them together with original passages of transition and explanations of things likely to be unfamiliar to his audience. Thus there are digressions on Old Testament dietary laws (11. 37–84), on angels appearing on horseback (11. 508–13), and on elephants (11. 564–73):

Sumum menn wile þincan syllic þis to gehyrenne,
for þan þe ylpas ne comon næfre on engla lande.
Ylp is ormæte nyten, mare þonne sum hus,
eall mid banum befangen, binnan þam felle,
butan æt ðam nauelan, and he næfre ne lið.

(To some men it will seem strange to hear this,
because elephants never come to England.
An elephant is an immense beast, greater than a house,
all surrounded with bones, within the skin,
except at the navel, and he never lies down.)

(*LS* XXV.564–68)

Ælfric's choice of the Maccabees for extended treatment seems to have been motivated by a more specific intention than the inculcation of the general lesson that service to God is best. Judas Maccabeus led a heroic revolt against his people's oppressors; England, suffering under the Danish attacks, needed a Judas Maccabeus, too. That lesson is, indeed, drawn explicitly by Ælfric at the end of his paraphrase:

Secgað swa-þeah lareowas þæt synd feower cynna gefeoht;
iustum, þæt is, rihtlic; *iniustum*, unrihtlic;
ciuile, betwux ceaster-gewarum; *Plusquam ciuile*, betwux siblingum.
Iustum bellum is rihtlic gefeoht wið ða reðan flot-menn,
oþþe wið oðre þeoda þe eard willað fordon.

(Nevertheless teachers say that there are four kinds of war;
justum, that is, just; *injustum*, that is, unjust;
civile, between citizens; *Plusquam civile*, between relatives.
Justum bellum is just war against the cruel seamen,
or against other peoples that wish to destroy [our] land.)

(*LS* XXV.705–09)

The summarized translation of Joshua which appears in the *Heptateuch* also deals with the subject of "just war." Nothing is known of the circumstances of its composition, except that Ælfric mentions in the *Letter to Sigeweard* that it was written at the request of Æthelweard (Crawford, 32). Moreover, the paraphrases of Judges, Esther, and Judith emphasize substantially the same point. All three tell stories of just wars waged by God's chosen people against their enemies. Of Judges, Ælfric says in the *Letter to Sige-*

weard, that it tells how the Hebrew nation, when it forsook God, was oppressed by "hæðenum leodum" (heathen peoples). But when they called upon God with true repentance, he sent them aid and they were delivered. In commenting on Esther and Judith in the *Letter,* he is even more explicit:

Seo ys eac on Englisc on ure wisan gesett
eow mannum to bysne, þæt ge eowerne eard
mid wæpnum bewerian wið onwinnendne here.

(It has also been put in English, in our manner,
for your instruction, so that you may defend your land
with weapons against a foreign army.) (Crawford, 48)

Dubois points out that Judith appears to be particularly addressed to a feminine audience, either nuns or widows who had taken a vow of chastity.[12] In praising Judith's chastity, he digresses to attack incontinency among nuns (1. 429); and, at one point, he directs his words to a female audience:

Ic wylle eac secgan, min swustor, þæt . . . clænnys micele mihte hæfþ.

(I also wish to say, my sister, that . . . purity has great power.)
(Assmann, 115)

Of the method employed in these epitomes, little need be said. Ælfric follows here the technique employed in his other paraphrases; he translates selected passages closely and connects them with original passages of summary, explanation and commentary. Dubois provides tables demonstrating, in some detail, the relationships between Ælfric's versions and the Vulgate text.[13]

VII *The Old English Pentateuch*

We come last to Ælfric's one venture into sustained translation in the generally accepted sense, as opposed to the rendering of incidental passages or to the making of paraphrases: his contribution to the so-called Old English Pentateuch. The circumstances under which Ælfric undertook this project are described in the preface to Genesis, one of the lengthiest and most interesting of Ælfric's English prefaces. The preface is addressed to Æthelweard, who had requested that he complete an already existing partial translation of Genesis:

Þu bæde me, leof, þæt ic sceold ðe awendan of Lydene on Englisc þa boc Genesis: ða þuhte me hefigtime þe to tiþienne þæs, and þu cwæde þa þæt ic ne þorfte na mare awendan þære bec buton Isaace, Abrahames suna, for þam þe sum oðer man þe hæfde awend fram Isaace þa boc oþ ende.

(You requested, sir, that I should translate from Latin into English the book of Genesis: I thought it burdensome to undertake this, and you told me that I need translate only to Isaac, Abraham's son, for someone else had translated from Isaac to the end of the book.) (Crawford, 76)

Ælfric then discusses in the preface the danger, in translating the Old Testament, that ignorant men will think that they can live now as the Patriarchs lived under the "Old Law." He also comments on the proper ways of interpreting the Old Testament and remarks on his techniques of translation.

Ælfric's translation of the first part of Genesis was incorporated, apparently in the eleventh century, into a compilation of Old English translations of the Pentateuch which was printed, in the seventeenth century, along with Ælfric's versions of Joshua and Judges, as the "Old English Heptateuch." This title is retained by its modern editor, S. J. Crawford, for his Early English Text Society edition of the works. Just how much of this composite translation of the Pentateuch is Ælfric's work is somewhat in doubt.[14] Most, if not all, of the translation was formerly attributed to him, but it now appears that the only portions by Ælfric are Genesis, chaps. 1–24 (with the exceptions of chapters 4–5 and 10–11), and Numbers, 13–26. Ælfric apparently did no more than fulfill his agreement to translate "as far as Isaac" in the Book of Genesis, but there is some evidence that he made minor revisions in the other man's translation of the rest of the book. As for the passage from Numbers, it appears to be part of a homily by Ælfric incorporated into the composite translation by the eleventh-century editor.

The Book of Genesis, with its account of the Creation and Fall, was of course one of the central parts of the Bible to Ælfric, as it is to all Christians; and he treated its contents in many forms. *De Temporibus Anni* and the *Hexameron* cover the Creation, relating it to the facts of the physical world; and the homiletic accounts of universal history, especially *De Initio Creaturae* (*CH* I. I), lay particular stress upon the Creation. There is reason to believe that Ælfric's translation of Alcuin's handbook on Genesis, the *Interrogationes Sigewulfi,* was written after the Genesis translation in order to supply the need for interpretation mentioned in the Genesis preface.[15]

In the translation itself, however, Ælfric confines himself for the most part to the aim he expresses in the preface:

We secgað eac foran to þæt seo boc is swiþe deop gastlic to understandenne, and we ne writaþ na mare butan þa nacedan gerecednisse.

(I say also in advance that the book is very deep in its spiritual meaning, and I write no more than the naked narrative.) (Crawford, 77)

He translates somewhat more closely and literally than he does in his other biblical versions. Within the twenty-four chapters he translated, the major omissions are chapters 4–5 and 10–11. Chapters 4–5 include the story of Cain and Abel, and chapters 10–11 the story of the Tower of Babel; but, for the most part, they consist of genealogies and apparently were regarded as expendable by Ælfric. These omissions have been supplied in the surviving manuscripts by other translators.

In addition to these large omissions, a number of smaller omissions and compressions of material occur. The list of Nahor's twelve sons is omitted, with a note that their names are in the Latin version: "let him who wishes read them there" (Crawford, 143). The same formula is used to pass over the account of Isaac's wife in Genesis 24:11–60. At another point he refuses to translate objectionable material:

Se leodscipe wæs swa bysmorful þæt hi woldon fullice ongean gecynd heora galnysse gefyllan, na mid wimmannum ac swa fullice þæt us sceamað hyt openlice to secgenne.

(The nation was so corrupt that they would foully satisfy their lust against nature, not with women but so foully that we are ashamed to say it openly.) (Crawford, 132)

The style of the translation up to chapter 19 is non-rhythmical, but the rhythmical style does begin to appear in it and is used consistently from chapter 22 on.

In general, the reservations Ælfric expressed in the preface about translating the Bible are implicit in the translation itself. Ælfric did his job conscientiously and thoughtfully, but he was too conscious of how the "naked narrative" could be misunderstood to translate freely and fully the Book of Genesis.

Ælfric's work as a Bible translator is full of paradoxes. On the one hand, he constantly expressed fears that his work would cause "the pearls of Christ to be held in disrespect"; on the other, he produced the largest, most impressive body of Bible translation in Old English. He apparently shared Jerome's conviction that even the individual word is sacred in Holy Scripture; and yet, he translated so freely that much of his work could be regarded as loose paraphrase. Although he says that he "dared write no more in English than the Latin has," he frequently adds passages in which he draws explicit morals from the biblical materials.

These paradoxes do not exactly amount to contradictions. They stem rather from difficulties inherent in the translation of sacred texts and from the very fact that Ælfric was too sophisticated and self-conscious a stylist to believe that a direct and literal-minded approach would resolve these difficulties. Like King Alfred, he knew that he had to "gather his own tools and his own timber" and to build the best house he could. The result was a series of clear, eloquent, and useful fragments; but Ælfric's own misgivings were too strong for it to be more.

CHAPTER 5

The Grammar *and the* Colloquy

ALL of Ælfric's works may be regarded as teaching pieces, in the broad sense of the word, addressed to the laity, as were the *Catholic Homilies,* or to the clergy, as were the *Lives of Saints*, the *Pastoral Letters,* and the *Life of Æthelwold.* But there is also a small group of works that Ælfric wrote specifically in his function as master of oblates at Eynsham for the instruction of his pupils: these include *De Temporibus Anni,* his treatise on chronology and astronomy; the *Grammar* and *Glossary;* and the *Colloquy.* These last works are closely related and perhaps deserve special emphasis for their intrinsic as well as their historical interest.

I *The* Grammar

Ælfric's *Grammar*, as its English preface indicates, followed soon after the *Catholic Homilies*, perhaps in 993–95. He issued it, as he did each volume of the *Catholic Homilies,* with a set of English and Latin prefaces; and he regarded it as closely related to his other works in his overall plan. Thus his English preface begins,

> Ic Ælfric wolde þas lytlan boc awendan to engliscum gereorde of ðam stæfcræfte, þe is gehaten *grammatica*, syððan ic ða twa bec awende on hundeahtatigum spellum, forðan ðe stæfcræft is seo cæg, ðe ðæra boca andgit unlicð.
>
> (I, Ælfric, wished to translate into English this little book of grammar, which is called *grammatica*, after I had translated two books of eighty sermons, because grammar is the key which unlocks the meaning of those books.)
>
> (Zupitza, 2)

The product of this work is of considerable historical interest because it is the first grammar of any language to be written in English. Apparently the work was fairly widely used, for it survives in fifteen manuscripts from scattered points of origin.[1] The *Grammar* not only provides some insights into Ælfric's pedagogic methods but also illuminates his understanding of the Latin language, his conception of its relations to English, and thus his principles of translation. It is also interesting linguistically because it contains one of the largest examples of a specialized technical vocabulary in Old English. Ælfric follows his sources rather closely in the content and arrangement of the books, and his chief original contribution is the invention of a complete set of English equivalents for the traditional terms of the Greek and Roman grammarians. Although, for historical reasons, his terminology did not become established as standard in later English grammar, his coinages demonstrate, as the theological terms of earlier Old English do also, the resources of Old English and its capacity for adaptation to a specialized use.

II *The Grammatical Tradition*

The study of grammar (by which was meant, of course, Latin grammar) was of fundamental importance in the Old English monastic school.[2] It formed the first subject in the so-called "trivium," and it was studied immediately after such preliminaries as learning the letters of the alphabet and the words of the *credo* and the *paternoster*. Only after the fundamentals of the Latin language were learned could the pupils proceed to rhetoric and dialectic and ultimately to the "quadrivium": music, arithmetic, geometry, and astronomy. In theory, at least, the pupils, after reaching a certain early stage, were supposed to speak only Latin, both in and out of school. We have no reason to believe that this rule was strictly enforced in tenth-century English schools, but Ælfric, in his instructional materials, emphasizes the vocabulary of everyday life and seems thereby to imply such an ideal. Despite his vernacular translations, Ælfric never questioned the necessity for a thorough grounding in Latin. His English translations, eloquent though they were, were to supply an immediate need, as had those of King Alfred; and Ælfric labored to insure that the next generation of the clergy would be able to read Latin texts better than his generation could. Grammar was the "key that unlocks the meaning of the books."

Ælfric inherited a double tradition of grammatical study: the "scientific" tradition of the Classical period and the pedagogical tradition of the more recent past.[3] Grammar had once implied the broad study of language in all its aspects, thereby encroaching upon the territories of metrics and the arts of poetry, rhetoric, and dialectics. Grammar had been the invention of the Greeks. Plato and Aristotle had both made contributions to grammatical theory: Plato had divided words into nouns and verbs, and sounds into vowels and consonants; and Aristotle had distinguished four parts of speech and remarked upon the tenses of verbs and the cases of nouns. Grammar was raised to the status of a methodical and important science, however, by the Stoic grammarians: Zeno of Citium (364–263 B.C.), Cleanthes of Assos (331–232 B.C.), and Chrysippus (280–208 B.C.). They established the major outlines of the study and, with the Alexandrian grammarians, the principal terminology. Greek grammar, in the version set forth by the major Alexandrian grammarian, Dionysius Thrax (born c. 166 B.C.), was adapted to the Latin language by M. Terentius Varro (116–27 B.C.); his *De Lingua Latina* established the main outlines of Latin grammar for centuries.

The grammars of the major Greek and Roman grammarians were not primarily pedagogical grammars. For the most part, they were written for native speakers of the language and were objective investigations of the nature and structure of language. The other grammatical tradition, the medieval pedagogical tradition, was a result of the extension of Latin geographically as the international language of learned discourse. Medieval grammars were written primarily to teach students a second language; therefore, they usually had a strongly practical, pedagogical emphasis.

The most influential figures in the shaping of medieval Latin grammar were Donatus and Priscian. Aelius Donatus, who lived in the fourth century, was the author of the *Ars Grammatica* and the *Ars Minor*. These grammars—the "greater Donatus" and the "lesser Donatus"—were the most widely used textbooks of the Middle Ages. To a great extent, they established the form of the Latin grammar studied throughout the Middle Ages and dictated the terminology of the grammars of most of the vernacular languages of Western Europe. Only slightly less prominent as a source of medieval grammar was Priscian (early sixth century), whose *Institutiones Grammaticae* was regarded as the standard advanced textbook to which the student progressed after mastering the more elementary Donatus. The popularity and wide dissemination of Priscian's

Institutes are suggested by the fact that it survives in more than a thousand widely distributed manuscripts. It continued to be used in schools through the Renaissance. Both Donatus and Priscian were in circulation in England very soon after the conversion.

The distinction of being the first English grammarian does not belong to Ælfric, although his is the first grammar in English. Bede, Tatwine, Boniface, and Alcuin had all written grammars of Latin for the instruction of English monastic pupils.[4] Bede's grammar, which survives in only fragmentary form, is brief and elementary; and it was probably intended as a first textbook for beginning students. Tatwine (d. 734), the author of Latin riddles, wrote a grammar which amounts to an expansion of Donatus's *Ars Minor*. Boniface (675–754), the Anglo-Saxon missionary to Germany, wrote a text called *De Partibus Orationis*, based like Tatwine's on Donatus. It includes model paradigms and long lists of examples which amount to glossaries embedded in the text. But the most interesting of early English grammars is the *De Grammatica* of Alcuin (735–804). Although brief, it is a witty, imaginative work which anticipates Ælfric's *Colloquy* as well as his *Grammar* in that it consists of a dialogue between a master and two students: Franco, a fourteen-year-old French boy, and Saxo, his fifteen-year-old English schoolmate. There are some elementary characterizations and entertaining asides in the little dialogue. For the grammatical content, Alcuin drew upon both Donatus and Priscian.

Ælfric's *Grammar* is a much more substantial production than any of these works by his English predecessors. His is a thoroughly practical, pedagogical text in the tradition of Donatus and Priscian; and it neither recalls the "scientific" tradition of the Classical grammarians nor anticipates the inclusive, anthologizing tendencies of later medieval grammarians. Ælfric's carefully composed work effectively adapts Donatus and Priscian to the needs and capacities of contemporary English pupils.

III *The Content and Arrangement of the* Grammar

Ælfric's *Grammar* is frankly based on both Donatus and Priscian. In the Latin preface, he writes, "I have endeavored to translate into your language these extracts from the Greater and Lesser Priscian for you, tender youths, so that, after reading through the eight parts of Donatus in this little book of mine, you can implant in your tender selves both languages, Latin and English, until you come to more advanced studies" (Zupitza, 1).

In general, the *Grammar* is organized on the plan of the *Ars Minor* of Donatus, but the major content, the definitions and examples, are drawn mainly from Priscian's *Institutes*. The "eight parts of Donatus" are, of course, the eight parts of speech, around which the *Grammar* is organized, following the *Ars Minor*. But Ælfric apparently conceives of his book as comparable in scope and difficulty to Priscian's, for which he expresses great admiration. Priscian, Ælfric declares, "is known as the ornament of all Latinity."

Despite the extent to which Ælfric draws upon Priscian and Donatus the *Grammar* is, by no means a mere pastiche of its sources. Ælfric strives throughout to clarify and simplify the material, to choose appropriate examples familiar to his English pupils, and to compare and contrast Latin with English.[5]

He also elaborates the fundamental plan of the book with "handbook" information and summaries that make it more useful. After the Latin and English prefaces, he begins with a series of brief explanations of basic terms—"voice," "letter," "syllable," and "diphthong" (4–8). He then includes a brief summary and definition of the parts of speech (8–11). This section is original with him and seems intended as an aid to beginning students who need a brief introductory overview of the subject before the detailed presentation begins. The definitions in this section are brief and informal, in contrast to the formal definitions later in the book, and are original with Ælfric. "Noun," for example, is defined as "the name by which we name everything, whether unique or common" (8). The examples given are from everyday English life, "Edgar" and "Æthelwold," for example, being used to illustrate proper nouns.

After these preliminaries, Ælfric begins the major section of the *Grammar*, a systematic presentation of the eight parts of speech (11–280). Beginning with the noun and progressing through the pronoun, verb, adverb, participle, conjunction, preposition, and interjection, he follows an orderly method of presentation. He first defines the part of speech carefully, giving an English equivalent for the Latin term. He then discusses subdivisions and subcategories of the part, and he finally treats its properties in some detail. In this central section of the book, Ælfric moves between Donatus and Priscian, sometimes acknowledging his source, more often not. An indication of his freedom in borrowing from both is his Latin definitions of the parts of speech. Donatus is drawn upon for the definitions of the verb, participle, and interjection, while Priscian contributes those of the pronoun and adverb. Ælfric writes original definitions of the conjunction and preposition, drawing upon both his sources. The book ends with three brief appendices of "useful facts": a list of the names of numerals; one of the "thirty divisions of grammatical art" from "voice" and "letter" to "fable" and "history"; and a brief postscript on money measures ("*Libra* on Leden is pund on Englisc," etc.).

Throughout the *Grammar*, Ælfric demonstrates a vivid sense of the needs, the capacities, and the interests of the "tender youths" to whom the book is addressed. He constantly simplifies and clarifies the material, but he does not compromise his aim of writing a fairly thorough text on about the level of Priscian's *Institutes*. His opening, simple summary and the clarity of his overall organization exemplify this intent, as does his practice of compressing or omitting material from Priscian of secondary importance. Thus he omits long sections of unnecessary examples in Priscian with a comment such as this:

Ða naman . . . synd *denominativa* gecwedene, and ðara ys fornean ungerim.

(Names . . . are called *denominativa,* and they are almost numberless.) (Zupitza, 18)

And thus he ends his section on the verb with,

Nelle we na swyðor her be ðam worde sprecan. Wel, gif ðis aht fremað.

(We will not speak any further here of the verb. It is well, if this benefits anything.) (Zupitza, 222)

Ælfric also freely substitutes his own examples for those of Donatus and Priscian. Sometimes he contributes examples that would be familiar to his students. Such schoolboy phrases as "ic write, wel he writ, yfele we raedað" (I write, he wrote well, we read badly), for example, are used to illustrate the adverb. In other cases, he chooses new examples in the interest of piety: saints' names, holy objects, or scriptural quotations. Names that end in *-eus* are illustrated by "Matheus se godspellere," for instance. Lawrence

Shook calls attention to an interesting treatment of Priscian's examples by Ælfric in the section on jurative adverbs (227).[6] Ælfric refuses either to use Priscian's Roman oaths (*Hercle* and *Mediusfidius*) or to substitute Christian ones. He briefly treats the preposition *per* as a jurative adverb in such phrases as *juro per deum* and *per meum caput,* quotes Christ's injunction to "Let your speech be yea, yea; no, no," and concludes,

Na syndon swergendlice *adverbia*, ac hwæt sceolon hi gesæde, nu we swerian ne moton?

(There are more swearing *adverbia*, but why say anything of them, since we must not swear?)
(Zupitza, 227)

Ælfric also goes beyond his sources in the attention he pays to English grammar and its relation to Latin. In the Latin preface, he hopes that his book will help his students "in both languages, namely Latin and English" (1); and, in the English preface, he similarly says that the book will be "sum angyn to ægðrum gereorde" (an introduction to both languages) (3). Throughout the work, he makes comments on English, which, though they do not amount to anything like a systematic grammar, do demonstrate his absorbing interest in his own language. Most of these comments center on the similarities and differences between the two languages. In discussing the letters of the alphabet, for example, he remarks that in addition to the vowels *a, e, i, o,* and *u,* the letter *y* is often used in names taken from Greek and that "this same *y* is very common in English" (5). He comments that the eight parts of speech apply to English as well as to Latin (11), that Latin does not have patronymic names, as English does (14–15), and that each language has its own untranslatable interjections (279–80).

IV *Ælfric's Grammatical Terminology*

One of the most interesting of Ælfric's original contributions to the *Grammar* is his creation of a complete set of grammatical terms in English.[7] The technical vocabulary of grammar is, of course, highly abstract and difficult to translate. Ælfric's English equivalents to the Latin terms illustrate not only the capacity of Old English to create new words to express involved concepts but also his own ingenuity and his mastery of both Latin and English. Throughout the *Grammar,* each time a new term is introduced, Ælfric translates it into English, usually thereby coining a new word: "*Pronomen* is ðæs namen speliend" (The *pronomen* is the noun substitute) (8), "*Nominativus* ys nemniendlic" (*Nominativus* is naming) (22), and so on. It is sometimes assumed that Ælfric meant to propose these English terms as replacements for the Latin terms, but he seems to have had no such intention. In only a few instances does he himself use the English term consistently in his subsequent discussions; more often he alternates between the Latin and English terms, even using the Latin terms somewhat more frequently. The English terms seem, in most cases, to be explanations of the Latin terms of the kind that a good teacher would provide to help his students understand and remember the new terms, not replacements for them.

Whatever Ælfric's intentions were, he did create a comprehensive set of English grammatical terms in the course of his translation. Probably some of these were already conventional in the classroom practice of his day; they seem inevitable and are probably not original with Ælfric. Most, however, reflect a consistent method and are undoubtedly Ælfric's inventions. A few are taken directly from Latin, such as "case" (Latin *casus*) and "part" (Latin *pars*). A much larger group simply employs already existing English words in new meanings: "had," "cynn," "tid," "name," and "word," for Latin *persona, genus, tempus, nomen,* and *verbum,* for instance.

Another large group of terms employs combinations of native words to render the meaning of the Latin terms. *Vocales*, for instance, is rendered "clypiendlice" (speakings) and *semivocales* is "healfclypiendlice" (half-speakings). Sometimes the product is a compound word or phrase. *Syllaba* becomes "stæfgefeg" (letter-combination), and *pronomen* becomes "naman speliend" (noun substitute). Often such compounds result from analysis and literal translation of each morpheme in the Latin terms. Thus *participium* (*parti* + *cip* =, from *capere,* "to take") is rendered "dæl nimend" (part-taking). The English term thus derived is usually precise, but is occasionally impossibly clumsy. *Interjectio*, for instance, is analytically translated "betwuxaworpennys" (between-throwing), an accurate enough rendering but a tongue twister, like "underðeodendlic" (under-joining) for *subjunctivus.*

Ælfric could hardly have meant to propose the regular adoption of such terms; they are explanatory renderings of the Latin terms, for teaching purposes. The only English terms that he himself uses regularly in preference to the Latin ones are such simple and natural substitutions as "tid" for *tempus,* "cynn" for *genus,* "word" for *verbum*, and "stæf" for *littera.*

Ælfric's vernacular grammatical vocabulary was one of the first such vocabularies for any European language. It did not, however, become established as the permanent English grammatical vocabulary. The Norman Conquest effectively ended the continuity of English scholarship; and, when the study of grammar in English was resumed centuries later, new translations of the Latin terms were made, which ultimately became standard. Thus we speak today of "letters" rather than "staffs," of "tense" rather than "tide," and of "gender" rather than "kind." Nevertheless, Ælfric's grammatical vocabulary provides a valuable insight into the resources of Old English as well as of his own as linguist and teacher.

V *The* Glossary

Appended to seven of the fifteen extant manuscripts of the *Grammar* is a Latin-English *Glossary* of several hundred words. This *Glossary,* probably by Ælfric and intended to accompany the *Grammar,* is not arranged alphabetically but by topics. There are eight sections. The first begins with *deus omnipotens* and gives the words for the major parts of God's creation: Heaven, the angels, the earth, the sea, and man. The second section—*Nomina membrorum*—names the "members" of the body, of society, and of the family. The last six sections take up the names of birds, fish, animals, plants, trees, and domestic items. The *Glossary* is of considerable value, of course, in the study of the Old English vocabulary; but it is not otherwise remarkable. Its contents and arrangement follow a familiar pattern in medieval texts; if Ælfric had any specific source, it was probably the *Etymologies* of Isidore of Seville.[8]

It does bear some relationship to both the *Grammar* and the *Colloquy*. The emphasis in the *Glossary* is strongly upon "everyday" words, ones that pupils would be likely to need in everyday life around a monastery, rather than words that would be needed in translating academic texts. It therefore shares the practical goals of the *Grammar* and suggests that Ælfric aimed at his pupils' mastery of Latin as an everyday, spoken language. The same goal is suggested by the earthy little *Colloquy*, the vocabulary of which is partially contained in the *Glossary*. The fact that some of the Latin terms in the *Colloquy* do not appear in the *Glossary* has led to the suggestion that Ælfric probably had several such lists and that he used the *Colloquy* in conjunction with another *Glossary* that was slightly different from the one that has been preserved.

VI *The Background of the* Colloquy

Ælfric's *Colloquy* is perhaps the most frequently reprinted and widely known of any of his works, rather paradoxically so since it is a slight piece, obviously dashed off to satisfy a pedagogical need. A short dialogue between a teacher and his pupils, it has the modest aim of offering practice in the Latin needed for use in everyday situations in a monastic school. There are good reasons for modern interest in it, however. For one, the Old English gloss offers a sample, admittedly little more than tantalizing, of Old English used in a sustained piece of dialogue. Old English literature has no drama; and, even in the narrative prose and poetry, dialogue is much rarer than it is in, say, the Icelandic saga literature, The *Colloquy* hardly offers anything approaching a genuinely creative, dramatic dialogue—its purpose is too limited and the gloss is too much bound by the Latin for that—but it does suggest, here and there, the movement of a genuine, conversational exchange, despite the classroom setting.

Its very humbleness of purpose gives the *Colloquy* an interest for us that Ælfric and the anonymous glossator of his work could hardly have anticipated. Its concentration on subjects and characters from everyday experience gives us a rare glimpse, brief as it is, of life in and around a tenth-century monastery—the everyday life that never enters the more exalted worlds of the Maldon poem or Ælfric's own passions of Roman martyrs. But, beyond these extrinsic considerations, the *Colloquy*'s "charm" (an overused word that, nevertheless, seems the right one) stems in large part from the skill and wit with which Ælfric executed his task. The little details of monastic life that appear in the dialogue and the pithiness of some of the exchanges reveal clearly a side of Ælfric's character that is partially suppressed in his larger works, though it crops out here and there: his earthiness, his common sense, and his sympathetic concern for the humbler members of society.

Ælfric's Latin text of the *Colloquy* is preserved, either in part or complete, in four manuscripts.[9] The best of these (British Museum, Cotton MS Tiberius A.iii) contains a continuous interlinear gloss in Old English. This gloss is not complete; at the beginning, each word is glossed; but, toward the end, words and phrases which have appeared before are left unglossed. Some attempt is made to use Old English word order, especially in short phrases; but the Latin word order naturally dominates the gloss. It was formerly believed that this text was only partially by Ælfric and that it had been amplified by one Ælfric Bata. There is no good reason, however, to suppose that the Latin portion of the Cottonian manuscript is not entirely by Ælfric. The confusion apparently arose because another manuscript (St. John's College, Oxford, Codex No. 154) contains an expanded version of the *Colloquy* with a rubric in which Ælfric Bata attributes the *Colloquy* to "my master Abbot Ælfric" and says that he himself has expanded it. This Ælfric Bata seems to have been a prolific writer of colloquies; the Oxford manuscript contains three more by him—and all, like his expansions of Ælfric's, are repetitive and pedantic. Nothing else is known of him except for a reference in Osbern's *Life of Dunstan* to an Ælfric Bata "who had tried to disinherit the Church of God." G. N. Garmonsway suggests that the nickname "Bata" may mean he was shortsighted, "whether literally or figuratively."[10]

The authorship of the Old English gloss is another matter. On the face of it, it would seem unlikely that Ælfric wrote it. The gloss of such a teaching piece would be only for the use of the teacher, and we can hardly imagine a Latinist of Ælfric's skill needing a gloss; but it is possible, of course, that it was circulated for the use of other teachers and that Ælfric provided an English gloss in the same way that he provided both Latin and English prefaces for his other books. The gloss is, however, by no means a model of the kind we would expect Ælfric to produce if this were his intention. Not only is it incomplete, it contains a number of errors and mistranslations. Furthermore, a number of words are glossed with Old English words different from those used in the *Glossary* to define the same words. *Sacerdos,* for example, is "sacred" in the *Glossary,* but "mæsse-preost" in the *Colloquy,* and *murenas* is "merenæddre" in the *Glossary*, but "lampredan" in the *Colloquy*. Neither of these arguments is conclusive; Ælfric may have made mistakes himself, and he may have glossed the same word differently at different times. As Garmonsway points out,[11] the *Glossary* is for the child; the

Colloquy, for the master. But the general implication of the admittedly imperfect evidence is that Ælfric did not write the gloss.

The fact that the pupils in the *Colloquy* introduce themselves as plowmen, herdsmen, merchants, etc., has sometimes led to misunderstanding. This introduction tells us, in fact, nothing of the "diffusion of education among all classes"; the pupils are merely assuming roles for the purpose of introducing certain kinds of vocabulary, closely related to the categories of the *Glossary*. Nor is the master a "secular," in spite of his apparent ignorance of monastic life; this pretense is also adopted so certain terms related to monastic life can be introduced. The classroom procedure was probably for the master to ask a series of questions like those in the *Colloquy* which encouraged the students to adopt a series of roles and to compose extemporaneous answers which employed a certain vocabulary. Ælfric may have had several such sets of questions; our text may be one which he wrote down and offered as a model. At early stages of instruction, the teacher may have provided specimen answers; the answers in the *Colloquy* may be intended in this way, or they may even, as Garmonsway suggests, be some of the best of his pupils' replies, which Ælfric himself edited.

This sensible and practical method of instruction was not original with Ælfric. A number of monastic colloquies survive from the Old English period, though Ælfric's is much the most readable of them. A number of them have been collected and edited by W. H. Stevenson.[12] These colloquies derive not from the superficially similar dialogues of Classical literature, but from the most popular Greek textbook of the Middle Ages, the *Hermeneumata Pseudo-Dositheana,* a compilation built around the *Ars Grammatica Dosithei Magistri*, a fourth-century grammar expanded by later writers with vocabulary lists, "readers," and, most relevant to our purposes, little Greek-Latin dialogues on homely subjects. These dialogues vary from manuscript to manuscript; apparently it was common practice for teachers to compose their own colloquies to use along with the grammar. At least two of the colloquies printed by Stevenson follow the colloquies of the *Hermeneumata* closely in content and arrangement.

It is perhaps unfair to evaluate such modest pieces by the standards of art, but the besetting defects of most of them are prolixity and dullness. Garmonsway has indicated some lively scenes in Bata's colloquies;[13] but, for the most part, the characters and their questions are the slightest of pretexts for the introduction of the long word lists which are sometimes clogged with recondite words which seem to serve no purpose but to demonstrate the authors' learning. The great virtues of Ælfric's *Colloquy* are its selectivity and economy. It introduces a good deal of vocabulary, but the word lists never swamp the characters and the simple situation. The conversation is given a dramatic quality in the differences of opinion that emerge, in the shifts in groupings of characters, in the liveliness of some of the thumbnail portraits, and in the unifying effect of a dominant theme.

VII *The* Colloquy

The setting of the *Colloquy* is a classroom, and the participants are a master and his pupils. The first two-thirds of the piece consists of a series of questions and answers concerning various occupations. The Cottonian manuscript contains few indications of speaker—none before the cook (1.194)—but it is never unclear who is speaking. The students begin by asking the master to teach them to speak Latin correctly:

> We cildra biddaþ þe, eala lareow, þæt þu tæce us sprecan forþam ungelærede we syndon and gewæmmodlice we sprecaþ.
>
> (We children beg you, O master, to teach us to speak [Latin correctly] for we are unlearned and speak badly.) (ll. 1–3)

The first speaker, who assumes the role of a monk, tells something of his daily routine: he sings seven services a day and is otherwise occupied with reading and singing (ll. 13–16). He introduces his fellow pupils, who will impersonate plowmen, shepherds, oxherds, hunters, fishermen, fowlers, merchants, shoemakers, salt-workers, and bakers.

The pupils, who then assume these roles in this order, are catechized about their lives. The result is a gallery of miniatures of characters from contemporary life; a comparison is inevitable with Chaucer's far more ambitious and complex gallery in the Prologue to the *Canterbury Tales*. Although most of the conversations are very brief—the longest are those of the hunter and the fisherman, which run to thirty-six lines each—most of them go beyond the immediate purpose of introducing vocabulary to suggest the motivations and the attitudes of the speakers. The plowman fears his master so much that he plows his acre a day even in a storm (11. 24–27); the shepherd has to work almost as hard in order to be faithful to his lord (11. 36–42).

The king's hunter also stresses his relation to his master, but with a somewhat different emphasis. After describing his methods of hunting with nets and hounds, he is asked what he does with his game; and he replies:

Ic sylle cynce swa hwæt swa ic gefo, forþam ic eom hunta hys.

(I give the king whatever I take, for I am his hunter.) (11. 81–82)

The king, in return, clothes and feeds him well, and sometimes gives him a horse or a ring, "so that I may pursue my craft more willingly" (11.84–85).

The dialogues of the fisherman and the merchant are used as an occasion to introduce lists of terms from the *Glossary* of the names of fish and of various wares, but such lists never become overwhelming. (In the Oxford text, Bata has expanded these lists and introduced new ones, which do become tedious, of animals, birds, trees, and plants.) Rather, the vocabulary is introduced easily and naturally in the course of the short interviews which emphasize not only the speaker's craft but also his personal attitudes. The plowman's wretchedness and servility are contrasted with the hunter's rather complacent recital of his skill and the rewards he receives for it. The fisherman is not above revealing a healthy respect for the sea and its dangers:

Wylt þu fon sumne hwæl?
Nic.
Forhþi?
Forþam plyhtlic þinge hit ys gefon hwæl. Gebeorhlicre ys me
faran to ea mid scype mynan, þænne faran mid manegum scypum
on huntunge hranes.

(Would you like to catch a whale?
Not I.
Why not?

Because it is a dangerous thing to catch a whale. It is safer for me to go to the river with my ship than to go with many ships to hunt whales.) (ll. 109–14)

Most of the speakers are proud of their crafts, and several insist rather strongly on their importance to society. The shoemaker insists that "not one of you could pass the winter were it not for my trade" (l. 174), and the cook, too, regards himself as indispensable (ll. 200–202). The merchant, the most prosperous of the speakers, is also the most vehement in insisting on his value to society:

Hwæt sægst þu, mancgere?
Ic secge þæt behefe ic eom cingce and ealdormannum and weligum and eallum follce.

(What say you, merchant?
I say that I am useful to the king and to ealdormen and to the wealthy and to all people.) (ll. 149–51)

The merchant then enumerates the goods he imports, emphasizing the risks and perils he undergoes. "Do you sell them here at the same price you bought them there?" asks the master (l. 162). "I do not," the merchant firmly replies, "What would I achieve by my labors then?" Eric Colledge has pointed out the prominence of this theme of just reward for labor in the *Colloquy*.[14] The hunter, the fisherman, the fowler, all emphasize the profit they seek by their labors. The fowler even describes how he frees his hawks in the spring and trains new ones in the fall in order to avoid the expense of feeding idle hawks through the summer. In this theme of profit, Ælfric is probably echoing Augustine's lively defense of commerce and profit in a similar dialogue in his commentary on Psalm 70: 15. The subject was, of course, much debated throughout the Middle Ages; and it received its fullest treatment in English literature in the fourteenth-century *Piers Plowman*.

The other thematic thread that runs through all the interviews is the defense that each speaker makes of the value of his craft to society, and this theme finally provides the major "dramatic action" of the *Colloquy* when a "wise counsellor" is introduced (l. 208). The master asks the counsellor, "Which of these trades seems to you the greatest?" The counsellor replies that the service to God is the greatest; and when pressed to name the greatest secular occupation, replies, "Eorþtilþ, forþam se yrþling us ealle fett" (Agriculture, because the farmer feeds us all) (1. 219). This reply immediately provokes an outburst from the smith, the fisherman, and the carpenter, who defend their own crafts, until the counsellor quiets them with a long speech which concludes,

Swa hwæðer þu sy, swa mæsseprest, swa munuc, swa ceorl, swa kempa, bega oþþe behwyrf þe sylfne on þisum, and beo þæt þu eart; forþam micel hynð and sceamu hyt is menn nellan wesan þæt þæt he ys and þæt he wesan sceal.

(Whatever you are, whether priest, or monk, or peasant, or soldier, practice yourself in this, and be what you are; because it is a great disgrace and shame for a man not to be willing to be that which he is, and that which he ought to be.) (11. 240–43)

The quarrel thus resolved, the *Colloquy* ends with a short interrogation of one of the pupils about his own routine. The pupil tells what he does during the day, what he eats and drinks, and where he sleeps. Ælfric permits himself a small schoolmasterish joke at the expense of the convention in the colloquies of introducing long lists when the master asks the pupil what he eats. The pupil replies with a list of foods (11. 288–89). "You are very greedy, to eat all that," the master replies; and the serious-minded pupil explains that he does not eat all this food at one meal. The master concludes with a short speech admonishing the pupils to be diligent and virtuous (11. 308–15).

It is easy to exaggerate the merits of the *Colloquy*. It remains a modest teaching-piece, despite the appeal of its little glimpses into humble life and its toying with lofty themes. But, in its combination of warmth and liveliness, it reveals very clearly a side of Ælfric's personality which we are likely to miss in his more formal works. Appropriately enough, as the most popular piece in elementary Old English readers, it is still, almost nine centuries later, being used regularly to help students learn a language.

CHAPTER 6

Ælfric's Style

HOMILIST, hagiographer, translator, linguist: Ælfric's work in all these roles reflects his mastery of English prose, and it is as a prose stylist that he is chiefly known. Modern study of Old English literature has quite naturally focused heavily upon the poetry, for the prose of the period is less clearly literary and has more often attracted the attention of historians than of literary students. Nevertheless, recent studies have made clear not only the considerable intrinsic interest of the best Old English prose but also its relevance to the later history of English literature.

The apex of the Old English poetic tradition, judging from the texts that survive, was the eighth century; it is probably correct to see a certain decline in the few later poems, as in *Maldon,* for example. But Old English prose was later in developing; it was not until the late ninth and tenth centuries that the language, in the hands of a few writers, became a medium capable of expressing complex ideas forcefully and clearly in sustained prose. The Norman Conquest, of course, abruptly ended most English writing in either poetry or prose; but the Old English prose masters apparently continued to exercise an influence still felt when English again became a literary medium. Thus we can speak of a "continuity of English prose" with more confidence than of a "continuity of English poetry," despite such phenomena as the fourteenth-century alliterative poems.[1]

Ælfric is the central figure in this blooming—comparatively late in the Old English period—of literary prose. Artificial as it may be, then, to consider style largely apart from content, Ælfric's prose style deserves particular emphasis and even separate consideration in a survey of his achievement; though we should perhaps speak instead of Ælfric's prose styles. Ælfric is best known for the "rhythmical style" of the *Lives of Saints* and later works, but a large part of his literary production—notably most of the *Catholic Homilies*—is in ordinary, non-rhythmical prose. This prose is very accomplished; and, though Ælfric seems to have gradually abandoned it in favor of the highly personal rhythmical prose of his later works, it may usefully be examined separately.

Ælfric seems to have adopted the rhythmical style at some point in the second series of *Catholic Homilies*. The early works—the first series of *Catholic Homilies, De Temporibus Anni,* the *Grammar,* the *Interrogationes,* and most of *Genesis*—are in ordinary prose. (In *Genesis*, the rhythmical style begins to appear in chapter 19 and becomes consistent in chapter 22.) Seven pieces in *Catholic Homilies* II are predominantly rhythmical: X (St. Cuthbert), XIV (The Passion of Our Lord), XVIII (SS. Philip and James), XIX (The Invention of the Cross), XX (SS. Alexander, Eventius, and Theodolus), XXI (On the Greater Litany), and XXXIX (St. Martin). Four others (XI, XII, XXVII, and XXXV) have rhythmical passages of various lengths. All of the saints' lives in *Lives of Saints* are rhythmical, though some of the supplementary pieces are not. After the *Lives,* Ælfric seems to have written exclusively in the rhythmical style, though since the style itself has been used often as chronological evidence, we are not certain of this.

I *Ælfric's "Ordinary Prose"*

All Ælfric's prose, rhythmical or not, is marked by certain characteristics: clarity, balance, and a carefully controlled variety of syntactic patterns. He expressed his stylistic ideal very clearly in the Latin preface to the second series of *Catholic Homilies:* "I have hastened to form this following book, according as the grace of God has guided me. I have tried to do this avoiding garrulous verbosity and strange expressions, and seeking rather with pure and plain words, in the language of their nation, to be of use to my hearers, by simple speech, than to be praised for the composition of skillful discourse, which my simplicity has never acquired" (*CH* II, p. 1).

This declaration need not be taken completely at face value, for it is a commonplace of early medieval rhetoric. Ælfric follows his predecessors in conceiving of style in terms of a contrast between *simplex locution* (simple speech) and *artificiosus sermo* (artificial discourse). He describes his own style as simple and disclaims any ambition to achieve an artificial elegance. In this respect, he follows, ultimately, St. Augustine, whose *De Doctrina Christiana* renounced the Sophistic rhetorical tradition to create a new, Christian rhetoric, based on Cicero and designed for preaching the word of God.[2] Ælfric, in describing his own stylistic goals, seems to echo such passages in *De Doctrina Christiana* as this: "He who teaches will rather avoid all words that do not teach. If he can find correct words that are understood, he will choose those; if he cannot, whether because they do not exist or because they do not occur to him at the time, he will use even words that are less correct, provided only the thing itself be taught and learned correctly."[3]

That such simplicity did not imply a sterile asceticism is elsewhere made clear by Augustine. The task of the preacher, like that of the Ciceronian orator, is *docere, delectare, movere* (to inform, to please, and to move). The preacher must instruct, but he must also charm and arouse the emotions. There is room, therefore, within the general framework of simplicity for a gradation of styles: *genus submissum, genus temperatum,* and *genus grande* (the plain, the middle, and the grand style), corresponding to the three tasks of the orator. The good preacher must move from one style to another, not to display his own skill, but to instruct, charm, and finally move his listeners with a grave and restrained eloquence. "I think I have accomplished something not when I hear them applauding, but when I see them weeping" (*De Doctrina Christiana,* XXIV).

We need not assume that Ælfric was consciously following Augustine's counsels in his own homiletic theory and practice. They had become part of the patristic rhetorical tradition, sometimes appearing as perfunctory commonplaces in the work of writers whose own styles were anything but Augustinian in spirit. (We may, for example, read Abbo of Fleury's remarks in the preface to his *Historia Sancti Eadmundi,* one of Ælfric's sources.) Ælfric's acknowledgment of the Augustinian ideal was, however, anything but perfunctory. His own style is marked by the clarity and restraint Augustine recommends, but it also has the resources to rise to the eloquence of the middle and grand styles when the subject and the purpose demand it.

These qualities are apparent in Ælfric's earliest prose, even before he turned to the rhythmical prose for which he is best known. As an example, we may take the following paragraph from the first homily in the first series of *Catholic Homilies,* "De Initio Creaturae." It will be remembered that this piece serves as a kind of general introduction to the double series and consists of a sweeping survey of universal history. Beginning with a lofty passage in praise of God (ll. 1–18), Ælfric continues with a summary of the

Book of Genesis (ll. 18–27). He then proceeds to the next pivotal events in Christian history: the life of Christ (ll. 279–315), the Crucifixion and Resurrection (ll. 316–44), and the Judgment to come (11. 344–52). In this particular passage, he is describing, with great brevity, the life of Christ. It is naturally therefore something of a set piece, and the entire homily is a particularly eloquent one, but it is not so elevated as to be atypical of Ælfric's prose at this time:

He wæs *buton synnum* acenned, and his lif was *buton synnum*. Ne *worhte* he þeah nane *wundra* openlice ær þan þe he wæs þrihtigwintre on þære menniscnysse; *þa siþþan geceas* he him leorningcnihtas; ærest twelf, þe we hataþ "apostolas," *þæt sind "ærendracan." Siþþan he geceas* twa and hundseofontig, þa sind genemnede "discipuli," *þæt sind "leorningcnihtas."* þa *worhte* he fela *wundra*, þæt men mihton *gelyfan* þæt he wæs Godes bearn. He awende wæter to wine, and eode ofter sæ mid drium fotum, and he gestilde windas mid his hæse, and he forgeaf blindum mannum gesihþe, and healtum and lamum rihtne gang, and hreoflium smeþnysse, and *hælu* heora lichaman; dumbum he forgeaf getingnysse, and deafum heorcnunge; deofolseocum and wodum he sealde gewitt, and þa deoflu todræfde, and ælce untrumnysse he *gehælde;* deade men he arærde of heora byrgenum to life; and lærde þæt folc þe he to com mid micclum wisdome; and cwæþ þæt nan man ne mæg beon gehealden, buton he rihtlice on God *gelyfe,* and he beo gefullod, and geleafan mid godum weorcum geglenge; he onscunode ælc unriht and ealle leasunga, and tæhte rihtwisnysse and soþfæstnysse.

(He was born without sins, and his life was all without sins. He worked no wonders openly, though, until he had been thirty years in the human state. Then he chose followers for himself; first twelve, whom we call *apostolas,* that is, "messengers." Then he chose one hundred and seventy-two, who are called *discipuli*, that is, "students." Then he worked many wonders, so that men might believe that he was God's son. He turned water into wine, and went over the sea with dry feet, and he stilled winds with his command, and he gave blind men sight, and the halt and lame good movement, and the leprous smoothness of skin, and health of their bodies; to the dumb he gave speech and to the deaf hearing; to the devil-possessed and the demented he gave sanity, and drove out the devils, and he healed all sickness; dead men he raised from their graves to life; and taught the people he met with great wisdom; and said that no man could be healed, unless he truly believed in God, and he be fulfilled and his faith adorned with good works; he shunned all evil and all falsehood, and taught righteousness and truthfulness.)

(*CH* I.I, 295–315)

This prose may justly be described as simple, but it is far from naive or uncontrolled. Ælfric's purpose is not, of course, to summarize the life of Christ: he is writing a panegyric, brief enough to fit into the overall plan of the homily. He chooses, therefore, to focus on the miracles; and the general movement of the passage is that of a list of parallel items. The structure of the passage is thus easy to follow, even when delivered orally. The style, too, with its short clauses, its parallelism, and its pronounced rhythms, is eminently suited to oral delivery.

The chief patterning device is repetition. The above italicized words demonstrate how close the pattern of verbal repetition is in the passage; it serves to create an effect of unity and coherence purely as sound, beyond its reinforcement of logical parallels. The first sentence employs the phrase "buton synnum" in successive clauses, which are, however, varied in construction. "Ne worhte he þeah nane wundra" (1. 296) is echoed a few lines later in "þa worhte he fela wundra" (1. 301). In other cases, key words are repeated in variously inflected forms: "Gelyfan," "gelyfe," and "geleafan," and "hælu," "gehælde," and "gehealden."

A fair amount of alliteration of a clearly deliberate kind also appears, though it is not worked into a regular pattern. Most often it is found within a single phrase, rather than in successive phrases as a link between them: "Ne *w*orhte he þeah nane *w*undra," "a*w*ende *w*æter to *w*ine," "*w*odum he sealde ge*w*itt," etc. Such uses of alliteration serve to reinforce what is perhaps the most prominent stylistic characteristic of the passage: the tendency of the prose to fall into pairs of short phrases or clauses balanced off against each other. It would be possible to arrange the passage to demonstrate this:

> He wæs buton synnum acenned / and his life wæs eal buton synnum.
> he onscunode ælc unriht and ealle leasunga / and tæhte rihtwisnysse and soþfæstnysse.

But such balancing is almost wholly syntactical; no such devices as alliteration or regular stress are consistently used to bind the pairs together. Nor are all the groups simple pairs; groups of three are introduced:

> deofolseocum and wodum he sealde gewitt,/
> and þa deoflu todræfde, /
> and ælce untrumnysse he gehealde.

The balance and parallelism of the passage, then, have nothing distinctive about them. They are used very skillfully, but not essentially differently from the way they are often employed in good prose of any language.

This one passage cannot fairly suggest the range of Ælfric's early style. The contents of the first series of *Catholic Homilies* run from methodical exposition of scriptural texts through straightforward narrative to such lofty and almost incantatory passages as the opening of the sermon quoted here, and Ælfric adjusts throughout his style to the task at hand. But, throughout its range, his style is marked by its clarity, the flexibility and consistency of its syntactic patterns, and its use of repetition, controlled rhythm, and frequent, though unpatterned, alliterative effects.

II *The "Rhythmical Style"*

The origins of Ælfric's rhythmical style have been the subject of much study. His models, both English and Latin; his purposes in adopting the style; and the principles upon which it is organized—all have attracted the attention of scholars. We may initially define his prose style as one built on a succession of two-stress phrases arranged in pairs linked by alliteration. It suggests the form of Old English alliterative verse, but it differs from the verse in that the rhythms of its two-stress phrases are much looser than those of the half-lines of verse, its use of alliteration is less strictly ordered, and its diction and tone are not those of verse.

We are clearly justified in regarding the rhythmical style as a prose style rather than a poetic style, though the tendency of early students of Old English was to regard it as debased poetry and thus as evidence of a presumed decadence in late Old English literature.[4] Furthermore, the style is not a particularly florid or mannered one, despite its comparative regularity and its capacity for intensification into an exalted eloquence where required. Ælfric's ideal remains the Augustinian one of "pure and plain words" and "simple speech" in his rhythmical as in his ordinary prose.

As we have seen, the rhythmical style begins to appear in certain items in the second series of *Catholic Homilies.* No sharp dividing line separates the rhythmical from the non-rhythmical style; there are transitional passages and to a certain extent the new style represents a development and a regularization of elements in Ælfric's earliest prose: the tendency toward paired phrases and the frequent alliteration. It has been suggested that, in adopting his rhythmical style, Ælfric was carrying a step farther his purpose, one implicit in his earliest works, of developing an English style comparable to good Latin prose. G.H. Gerould has suggested that the immediate inspiration for the rhythmical style was the highly artificial Latin "rhymed prose" of a number of Ælfric's sources, including Augustine, Jerome, Ambrose, Sulpicius Severus, Gregory of Tours, and Bede.[5] This "rhymed prose" was characterized by a heavy use of rhyme, parallelism, antithesis, alliteration, and, especially, rhythmical final clauses. The *cursus*, as the rhythmical final clause was called, had three major types, each involving two stresses and a set number of unstressed syllables: *cursus planus* (/ x x / x), *cursus tardus* (/ x x / x x), and *cursus velox* (/ x x \ x / x). Gerould believes that Ælfric imitated the *cursus* as it appeared in his sources very closely: "These rhythmic endings, along with the alliteration, explain why Ælfric's sentences have a flow that has hitherto been usually taken for the flow of verse. The cadence is wholly a matter of the endings, I believe."[6] He regards Ælfric's alliteration as an attempt to capture with a native substitute the effect of rhyme in his sources.

Gerould does not insist upon his belief that Ælfric's stylistic devices are so closely modeled upon Latin ones. He is chiefly concerned, he says, "to point out that Ælfric was writing prose of a studied sort rather than clumsy and formless verse." This point is a valuable one, as is the general one that Ælfric was accustomed to a heightened, semipoetic prose in his sources and may well have consciously sought to produce similar effects in his own language.

Dorothy Bethurum,[7] though generally agreeing with Gerould's treatment of Ælfric's style as ordered prose, opposes his conclusion that Latin rhymed prose was its principal inspiration. She believes his major models to be English: "Although Ælfric's lines are not the lines of classical Old English poetry and can not be scanned by its rules, they are composed under its aura, and their rhythm approximates that of the heroic poetry more closely than it approximates anything else. . . . He was undoubtedly inspired by the Latin rhymed prose, was sensitive to its effects, and tried to produce in English something comparable to them. But his rhythm was an English rhythm, arrived at in an English fashion and not in a Latin." The question has implications beyond the limits of style, for Miss Bethurum believes that Ælfric's prose was so reminiscent of heroic verse that it would have suggested to his audience a connection between his Christian saints and the old Germanic heroes.

We are probably safe in concluding, with Miss Bethurum, that Ælfric wanted to create an English prose comparable in effect to the heightened Latin of many of his sources and that, to do so, he drew upon the poetic devices of his own language. Gerould's correspondences between the Latin devices and Ælfric's are not very exact, and Ælfric was probably too conscious that every language has its "agene wisan" to attempt any such literal imitation as Gerould suggests.

Ælfric was not alone in seeking a heightened English prose style: we may add to Latin rhymed prose and Old English heroic verse, as models for his style, earlier English prose, especially homiletic prose.[8] The Blickling homilies and those of the Vercelli Book have passages which make heavy use of rhythm and alliteration. The anonymous Life of St. Chad, which its most recent editor dates about 850, similarly anticipates Ælfric in its poetic effects, as does the so-called Old English Martyrology, from about the same time. Even the Alfredian translations (except, perhaps, the Orosius) are highly alliterative in certain passages. The sermons of Wulfstan continue the tradition after Ælfric.

Nevertheless, Ælfric's rhythmical style, while comparable to the styles of earlier homilists and to Wulfstan's, differs from all of them. He uses his own kind of two-stress word-groups and alliteration much more regularly and consistently than any of his predecessors, as nearly as we can judge from the extant texts; and his practice differs radically from Wulfstan's, whose basic unit is the single two-stress word-group rather than the linked pairs of word-groups Ælfric uses. His style is, indeed, so distinctive that its appearance in a text is almost certain evidence of his authorship.

The principles of the style have recently been clarified by a number of scholars, including Angus McIntosh, J. C. Pope, and Peter Clemoes;[9] and the comments that follow are closely based upon their conclusions. The first appearance of rhythmical prose in Ælfric's work should suggest his reasons for adopting it, but the items in *Catholic Homilies* II in which it is first used do not seem clearly different from those in the ordinary style. Peter Clemoes has tentatively suggested that he may have begun to use it for material which demanded an unusually elevated style, such as the narrative of the Passion (*CH* II.XIV).[10] In its formal patterns, the style suggested the order and universality of his themes: "The rhythmical style is the language of the spirit. It is transcendental. The unity of its interrelated, regular sound is the artistic counterpart of the unity of an interrelated, regular universe."[11] Some such intention must have led Ælfric to adopt the rhythmical style initially; but it is interesting to note that, once he adopted it, he apparently used it for all purposes and for all kinds of material. Not only sermons and saints' lives but private letters and occasional pieces are in the rhythmical style. Of course, the works that have survived, even the "private" letters, are of a rather formal character. And, as McIntosh comments in connection with Wulfstan's apparently habitual use of his own rhythmical style, in an age in which even private reading was done aloud, there was no occasion for which a strongly oral, rhythmical style would have been inappropriate.[12]

Of the first works in the rhythmical style, the homily on Cuthbert (*CH* II.X) is one of the most interesting, not only for its subject but because its rather hesitant and inconsistent style suggests that it may be one of Ælfric's first attempts in the new rhythmical form. The following passage tells of Cuthbert's decision to leave the monastery at Lindisfarne and to retreat into seclusion on the tiny island of Farne:[13]

Cuþberhtus se halga sippan gefremode
mihtiglice wundra on þam mynstre wunigende.
Begann þa on mode micclum smeagan,
hu he þæs folces lof forflean mihte,
þy læs þe he wurde to hlisful on worulde,
and þæs heofenlican lofes fremde wære.
Wolde þa anstandende ancerlif adreogan,
and on digelnysse eallunge drohtnian:
ferde þa to Farne, on flowendre yþe.
Þæt igland is eal beworpen
mid sealtum brymme, on sæ middan,
þæt wiþinnan eall ær þam fyrste
mid sweartum gastum swiþe was afylled,
swa þæt men ne mihton þa moldan bugian
for þeowracan sweartra deofla
ac hi ealle þa endemes flugon,
and þæt igland eallunge rymdon
þam æþelan cempan, and he þær ana wunode,
orsorh heora andan þurh ælmihtigne God.

(Cuthbert the holy afterward worked
mighty wonders living in the minster.
Then he began often to meditate
how he might flee from those people's praise
lest he become too famous in the world
and be estranged from heavenly praise.
He wished to take up an anchorite's life
and in solitude solely to live;
he fared then to Farne in the flowing waves.
That island is all surrounded
with salty surf, in the midst of the sea,
and within, it was all from long ago
completely inhabited by dark spirits,
so that men could not live on the land
for dread of the dark devils;
but they all fled together,
and gave up the island completely
to the noble champion and he lived there alone,
safe from their anger through almighty God.)

(*CH* II.X,142)

The general principles upon which the passage is organized are fairly obvious upon even a cursory inspection, although the details of their application may present some problems. The sentences tend to fall into short phrases, usually with two stresses each. The syntax establishes these phrases, which resemble the half-lines of alliterative verse. They are, however, much less rigorously controlled than the half-lines of verse; an indeterminate number of unaccented syllables may appear in any position around the two major stresses. Secondary stresses may appear also, as in "ancerlif adreogan" (1. 7). In this brief passage, the number of syllables in each phrase ranges from four (as in "pæt igland is") to eight (as in "on þam mynstre wunigende"). The average for these thirty-eight phrases is almost six. McIntosh has found an average of seven syllables per phrase in the Life of St. Oswald (XXVI),[14] and Pope reports that this average is accurate for most of Ælfric's later prose.[15] The early pieces in the rhythmical style, however, tend to use shorter phrases. Even so, however, Ælfric's phrases are longer than the half-lines of the poets: *Beowulf*'s half-lines average less than five syllables. The range is greater, too; the range from four to eight in this passage is typical, though Pope reports a few lines of three syllables and a few of eleven or twelve.

The two-stress groups are linked in pairs by syntax and by alliteration, again in much the manner of alliterative verse. There need not be a caesura between the members of a pair, and often there is not; a pause is more likely to come after a pair, at the end of a full "line." The variety in the number of syllables in the two-stress phrases, combined with this tendency toward end-stopped lines with light medial caesuras, if any, might suggest that Ælfric's basic unit is the full, four-stress "line," rather than the two-stress phrase. But, though it is true that a sense of the full line is stronger in Ælfric than in most of the verse, the syntactic groups are clear enough, even without caesura, to establish the two-stress phrase as the basic unit.

The basic pattern of alliteration is similar to that used by the poets; but, like the rhythmic pattern, it is much looser. Brandeis has found that about two-thirds of Ælfric's lines alliterate according to the standards of Old English verse.[16] That is, with one alliterative sound, they alliterate *aa:ax, ax:ay,* or *xa:ay*. With two, they alliterate *ab:ab* or *ab:ba*. The other third, however, vary widely, from lines with no alliteration at all to lines in which all four stresses participate in the alliteration. The Cuthbert passage offers examples of some of the more common patterns:

aa : ax

*f*erde þa to *F*arne, on *f*lowendre yþe

ax : ay

mid *s*ealtum brymme, on *s*æ middan

xa : ay

Begann þa on *m*ode *m*icclum smeagan

ab : ab

*m*ihtiglice *w*undra on þam *m*ynstre *w*unigende

Three lines (1, 6, and 15) lack alliteration. Brandeis estimates that about ten percent of Ælfric's lines are not alliterative, though Pope points out that, if we admit alliteration of minor syllables, the figure may be reduced to about three per cent.[17]

The phonetic conventions of Ælfric's alliteration are similar to those of the poets. All vowels may alliterate with one another; consonants generally demand exact correspondence. Ælfric deviates from the practice of the poets chiefly in allowing *s, sc, sp,* and *st* to alliterate with one another and in allowing *hl* to alliterate with either *h* or *l*. As in *Beowulf, hr* may alliterate with either *h* or *r*. (In line 5, above, "læs" alliterates with "hlisful.") Other conventions peculiar to Ælfric have been suggested by Schipper and Brandeis, but Pope points out that evidence for them is not conclusive.[18]

The rhythms and the alliterative patterns are, then, much like those of Old English verse, though considerably freer. That the passage clearly has the effect of prose rather than verse is the result not only of the looser patterning, but also of the essentially prosaic tone and diction. Ælfric draws upon the highly developed body of Old English poetic diction very rarely and then only for carefully controlled effects, as when, in line 18 of this passage, he suggests with the poetic formula "þam æþelan cempan" the conventional Christian imagery of the "warrior of Christ." His prose frequently rises in tone to poetic effects, but it usually does so through a tightening of the regular controls into greater rhythmic and alliterative regularity, as in line 9, "ferde þa to Farne, on flowendre yþe," which uses no "poeticisms" but forms two regular poetic half-lines.

Attention to the rhythmical elements should not obscure the extent to which the prose continues to use devices of unity and coherence prominent in the earlier prose: repetition, parallelism, and balance over larger sections than the two-stress phrase. These devices are less prominent in such narrative passages as the Cuthbert piece than in expository passages, but even here the sentence beginning with line 3 is formed around the antithesis of "folces lof" and "heofenlican lofes." Line 10 is closely echoed in line 17, and lines 13 and 15 use repetition with slight variation in "sweartum gastum" and "sweartra deofla." The entire passage, which forms a small unit, begins and ends with brief summarizing statements.

It is difficult to reconstruct the effect of such a style, so imperfect is our knowledge not only of the sounds and stress patterns of Old English but also of the contemporary connotations of such devices as alliteration. But it seems clear that Ælfric's style is a remarkable combination of freedom and restraint; that it is capable of clear, ordered exposition and narrative; and that it is flexible enough to rise easily and naturally to greater eloquence.

III *The Style of the "Passion of Saint Edmund"*

The full range of Ælfric's style can be demonstrated by an examination of one of his most polished works, the "Passion of Saint

Edmund, King and Martyr" (*LS* XXXII). This piece, it will be remembered, is a radical adaptation of a Latin life by Abbo of Fleury and seems, perhaps more than any other of Ælfric's works, to exploit reminiscences of Germanic epic in order to present Edmund's life as the material for a "Christian epic." The exact date of its composition is unknown, but Clemoes suggests that it must be one of the early *Lives* because Ælfric says he wrote it "within a few years" of 985, when Abbo and Dunstan met.[19] Whatever its date, its style shows the full development of the rhythmical form with which Ælfric seemed to be experimenting in the life of Cuthbert. It is also interesting in the range of styles it uses, from formal panegyric to straightforward narrative and exposition to impassioned exhortation.

The "Passion of Saint Edmund" begins with a prefatory note in non-rhythmical prose in which Ælfric explains the transmission of the story of Edmund's martyrdom from his sword-bearer, a witness, to King Æthelstan and Dunstan to Abbo of Fleury. With line 13, however, as he begins the life itself, he adopts his highest manner for an opening panegyric:

Eadmund se eadiga,   eastengla cynincg,
wæs snotor and wurðfull   and worðode symble,
mid æþelum þeawum,   þone ælmihtigan god.

(Edmund the blessed,   king of the East Angles,
was wise and honorable   and ever glorified,
by his noble ways,   almighty God.

(*LS* XXXII.13–15)

This passage, which extends to line 25, comes very close to alliterative verse in the regularity of its rhythms and its alliterative patterns. All six of the two-stress phrases quoted conform rhythmically to poetic practice; they could be classified according to the Sievers types or analyzed, in modern terms, as dactylic feet. The alliteration is equally regular; of these thirteen lines, four alliterate *xa: ay;* three, *ax: ay;* and two, *aa: ay*. The other four have double alliteration: three, *ab:ba;* one, *ab:ab*. The syntactic structure of the passage is highly formal; three parallel sentences recite Edmund's virtues:

Eadmund se eadiga, eastengla cynincg,
wæs snotor and wurðfull . . .
He wæs ead-mod and geþungen . . .

(He was humble and devout . . .)

(*LS* XXXII.16)

He wæs cystig wædlum and wydewum swa swa fæder.

(He was bountiful to the poor and to widows like a father.)

(*LS* XXXII.22)

With line 26, Ælfric's manner changes abruptly as he begins the narrative portion of the life. The arrival of the Danes, the exchange of messages between Hingwar and Hubba and Edmund, the martyrdom of the king, the miraculous recovery of his severed head, and his posthumous miracles are all described in a rhythmical, but less exalted, style. The rhythm and alliteration are still comparatively regular, but the stiffness of the opening rhetoric is relaxed and the two-stress phrases are looser in their syllabic structure:

Hinguar þa becom to east-englum, rowende,
on þam geare þe Ælfred æðelincg an and twentig geare wæs,
se þe west-sexena cynincg siþþan wearð mære.

(Hingwar then came to East Anglia, rowing,
in the year that the noble Alfred was twenty-one years old,
he who later became the great West-Saxon king.)

(*LS* XXXII.36–38)

Ælfric follows his usual practice of telling the story in strict chronological order, separating it into short episodes, each introduced by "þa" (then).

The style rises within this middle section of narrative most notably in the series of set speeches by Edmund and Hingwar's messenger (11. 43–93). Edmund's reply to his bishop who counsels submission deserves quotation:

Þæs ic gewilnige and gewisce mid mode,
þæt ic ana ne belife æfter minum leofum þegnum,
þe on heora bedde, wurdon mid bearnum and wifum,
færlice ofslægene fram þysum flot-mannum.
Næs me næfre gewunelic þæt ic worhte fleames,

ac ic wolde swiðor sweltan, gif ic þorfte,
for minum agenum earde, and se ælmihtiga god wat
þæt ic nelle abugan fram his biggengum æfre
ne fram his soþan lufe, swelte ic lybbe ic.

(This I desire and wish in my mind,
that I should not be left alone after my dear thanes,
who in their beds, with children and wives,
have suddenly been slain by these seamen.
It was never my way to take to flight,
but I would rather die, if I must,
for my own land, and the almighty God knows
that I will never turn aside from his worship
nor from his true love, whether I die or live.)

(*LS* XXXII.74–82)

This eloquent epic speech achieves its effect not through an abrupt change of style or through the employment of traditional heroic verbal formulas, but through the tightening and intensification of the controls operating through the less exalted prose. The two-stress phrases become slightly more regular and economical in their syllabic content, the alliteration is handled with great care, and logical and syntactic groups are balanced off against each other rather more strictly than usual.

The style is similarly elevated at the end of the life (11. 250–76) when Ælfric matches the opening praise of Edmund with a panegyric of all the English saints (the passage quoted in chapter 4). The life of Edmund is not thoroughly representative of Ælfric's mature rhythmical style because of its unusual eloquence. Much of Ælfric's rhythmical writing was more prosaic, but the life does exhibit very clearly the general characteristics of the style and its capacity for elevation. It is unusual only in its exceptional regularity. Pope [20] has analyzed its alliterative patterns in detail and found that of the 262 rhythmical lines (after the prefatory note), 246 alliterate regularly on the principal stressed syllables. A good number of them follow the strict practices of the "classical" Old English poets. Of the remaining sixteen lines, only two (151 and 193) lack any link between halves, and one of these is an exceptional line which imitates the cries of Edmund's head guiding the searchers:

Her, her, her; and swa gelome clypode
(Here! here! here! and so it often cried out.)
(1. 151)

It is difficult to be certain about the reasons Ælfric adopted the rhythmical style, his own conception of it, or the impression it made on the contemporary audience. But its general effect and its relation to Ælfric's ideas and attitudes seem clear. It is analogous artistically to the graphic arts of his time; the drawings in such a work as the Benedictional of St. Æthelwold, executed during Ælfric's lifetime at his own monastery at Winchester, have something in common with his style. They are simple and symmetrical in design, often partly or wholly in outline. They make no attempt at literal, realistic representation; the lively and meticulously executed detail with which the basic designs are elaborated is ornamental, not realistic. The effect is that of a serene, generalizing art in which the individual detail is subordinated to the general purpose of presenting universal subjects with a lightly ornamented simplicity.

Ælfric's prose is like these drawings in its highly patterned clarity and simplicity. Its patterns are not so rigid as to be constricting, and it is capable of emotional effects, as we have seen. But it functions as a distancing device; its orderliness is a continual reminder of the universal order of which Ælfric writes, and the particular detail, the individual subject, is always seen from a universal perspective through the generalizing effect of the style.

In Ælfric's style, the major elements of tenth-century English culture meet: the clarity and serenity of the Classical tradition as it was transmitted to him through his Latin sources, the universal vision of his Christianity, and the native strength of the Germanic heritage. In this sense, Ælfric's style perfectly reflects the general qualities of his personality and his art. It is difficult for the modern reader, even if he is fluent in Old English, to penetrate the barriers which the passage of time and the shifts in assumptions and values have raised between Ælfric's time and ours and to gain a sense of the man himself. Compared with other Old English writers, he left a remarkably large body of work; but the nature of that work, the conventions of his time, and, we may suspect, Ælfric's own disposition made his work largely impersonal; the man himself is revealed only occasionally and only indirectly.

The keynote of Ælfric's work is didacticism, though in the very highest sense of that often pejorative word. Ælfric was above all a teacher—most immediately of the young students in the monastic school, then of the congregations to whom he preached, and finally of the English nation itself. His entire work is unified by its educational purposes. Beginning with a broad survey, in the *Catholic Homilies* and in the *Lives of Saints,* of the basic teachings of the church most necessary for laymen, he went on to provide, in the pastoral letters and other works, the knowledge priests and monks needed to carry out their work, and in the materials for Latin instruction, the means for raising the level of learning in the next generation. He seems to have been very conscious of the coherence of his work as a whole and was fond of listing his books in his prefaces and letters and of reorganizing and revising earlier pieces, such as the *Catholic Homilies*.

This desire to lead others to knowledge informs not only his work as a whole but each of its parts as well. The good teacher's desire always to be understood, for example, led Ælfric to his persistent striving for absolute clarity. Although most of his writings were translations and adaptations, we can see his mind at work behind each of them as he prunes, rearranges, and explains in order to make the material perfectly clear to his audience. His pedagogical sense of his audience's interests and needs led him also to his constant awareness of the time and place in which they lived. This concern found expression not only in such things as his rendering of Old Testament terms into homely contemporary equivalents and as his emphasizing English saints in the *Lives,* but more importantly, in the way such contemporary facts as the Danish invasions, the series of crises in leadership, and the efforts of the monastic leaders to revive learning shaped Ælfric's choices and emphases in his material. He seldom mentions contemporary events, but such themes as the righteousness of a "just war" of self-defense, the qualities of the Christian king, and the strength that God lends his people in their time of need recur again and again in his work. The teacher's sense of responsibility for the accuracy and authority of his material, too, lies behind Ælfric's care in selecting his sources, his regular practice of seeking the endorsement of his superiors, and his attempts to prevent later writers from distorting his work or destroying its integrity.

Although it is as a stylist—as the first major writer of English prose—that Ælfric is chiefly remembered, his commitment to the service of God through the teaching of his countrymen gave his prose its power and purpose. Its variety, its clarity, and its rhythmic strength are the perfect expression of the quiet devotion and the gentle humanity of its author.

Notes and References

Chapter One

1. There are a number of general histories and surveys of the Old English period. The fullest and most authoritative is Sir Frank Stenton, *Anglo-Saxon England,* Vol. II of the *Oxford History of England* (2nd ed., Oxford, 1947). Briefer are Peter Hunter Blair, *An Introduction to Anglo-Saxon England* (Cambridge, 1956) and D. P. Kirby, *The Making of Early England* (New York, 1968). Dorothy Whitelock, *The Beginnings of English Society* (Penguin, 1952) is sound, readable, and available in paperback. Her *Changing Currents in Anglo-Saxon Studies* (Cambridge, 1958) is a helpful supplement.

2. For a full account of the Romans in Britain, see R. G. Collingwood and J. N. L. Myres, *Roman Britain and the English Settlements,* Vol. I of the *Oxford History of England* (2nd ed., Oxford, 1937).

3. This important excavation is described and illustrated in C. Green, *Sutton Hoo: The Excavation of a Royal Ship Burial* (London, 1963).

4. See P. E. Schramm, *A History of the English Coronation* (Oxford, 1937), and H. R. Loyn, "The King and the Structure of Society in Late Anglo-Saxon England," *History,* XLII (1957), 87–100.

5. The poem has been edited by E. V. Gordon for Methuen's Old English Library (London, 1937). A good study of the background of the battle is E. D. Laborde, *Byrhtnoth and Maldon* (London, 1936).

6. In addition to the general works cited in Note 1, see, on the monastic reform, Dom David Knowles, *The Monastic Order in England* (2nd ed., Cambridge, 1949), M. Deanesly, *Sidelights on the Anglo-Saxon Church* (London, 1962), and R. R. Darlington, "Ecclesiastical Reform in the Late Old English Period," *English Historical Review*, LI (1936), 385–428.

7. *King Alfred's West-Saxon Version of Gregory's Pastoral Care*. Ed. and trans. Henry Sweet. Early English Text Society, OS 45 and 50 (London, 1871–1872), pp. 3–4.

8. See, on Dunstan, J. A. Robinson, *The Times of St. Dunstan* (Oxford, 1923) and E. S. Duckett, *St. Dunstan of Canterbury* (London, 1955).

9. For Æthelwold, see, in addition to the titles cited in Notes 6 and 8, H. W. Heim, "Æthelwold und die Mönchreform in England," *Anglia,* XLI (1917), 405–43.

10. Chapter 6 of Duckett, *St. Dunstan of Canterbury,* is devoted to Oswald.

11. *St. Dunstan of Canterbury*, p. 111.

12. Two useful summary treatments of the subject are Wilfrid Bonser, "Survivals of Paganism in Anglo-Saxon England," *Transactions of the Birmingham Archaeological Society*, LVI (1939), 37–70, and F. P. Magoun, Jr., "On Some Survivals of Pagan Belief in Anglo-Saxon England," *Harvard Theological Review*, XL (1947), 33–46.

13. See the sermon "On Auguries" (*LS*, XVII).

14. Useful general studies of Anglo-Saxon Christianity are M. Deanesly, *The Pre-Conquest Church in England* (2nd ed., London, 1963), and John Godfrey, *The Church in Anglo-Saxon England* (Cambridge, 1962).

15. See J. Ryan, *Irish Monasticism* (Dublin, 1931).

16. Christopher Dawson, *Religion and the Rise of Western Culture* (New York, 1950).

17. Clinton Albertson, "Anglo-Saxon Literature and Western Culture," *Thought*, XXXIII (1958), 111–12.

18. The identity of Ælfric and the basic chronology of his life and works were first set forth by Edward F. Dietrich in Neidner's *Zeitschrift für die Historische Theologie*, XXV (1855), 487–594, and XXVI (1856), 163–256. The other basic accounts are Caroline L. White, *Ælfric: A New Study of His Life and Writings*, Yale Studies in English, II (New Haven, Conn., 1898) and Marguerite-Marie Dubois, *Ælfric: Sermonnaire, Docteur et Grammairien* (Paris, 1943). A recent authoritative reconsideration of the chronology is Peter Clemoes, "The Chronology of Ælfric's Works," in *The Anglo-Saxons: Studies in some Aspects of their History and Culture Presented to Bruce Dickens* Ed. Peter Clemoes (London, 1959), pp. 212–47. The account here given is based closely on these studies.

19. Dubois, *Ælfric*, p. 32.

20. See Francis Wormald, *English Drawings of the Tenth and Eleventh Centuries* (London, 1952). Wormald has also prepared a facsimile edition of *The Benedictional of St. Ethelwold* (London, 1959).

21. On Anglo-Saxon monastic life, see Knowles, *The Monastic Order in England*, and John C. Dickinson, *Monastic Life in Medieval England* (New York, 1962).

22. See Knowles, *The Monastic Order in England*, pp. 448 ff., upon which the timetable below is based.

23. On monastic schools, see in addition to the books cited in Note 21, A. F. Leach, *The Schools of Medieval England* (London, 1915), pp. 31–95.

24. J. Kemble, *Codex Diplomaticus Aevi Saxonici*. 6 vols. (London, 1839–1848), item 656. See also P. H. Sawyer, *Anglo-Saxon Charters* (London, 1968), item 1217.

25. *The Chronicle of Æthelweard*. Ed. and trans. A. Campbell (London, 1962).

26. See, for the best expression of this view, Peter Clemoes, "Ælfric," in *Continuations and Beginnings: Studies in Old English Literature*. Ed. E. G. Stanley (London, 1966), pp. 182ff.

27. "The Chronology of Ælfric's Works." (See Note 18.)

28. Kemble, *Codex Diplomaticus,* item 714. See also Sawyer, *Anglo-Saxon Charters,* item 911.

29. White, *Ælfric: A New Study,* p. 152.

30. D. J. V. Fisher, "The Early Biographers of St. Ethelwold," *English Historical Review,* LXVII (1952), 381–91.

31. Clemoes, "The Chronology of Ælfric's Works," p. 242.

32. Clemoes, "The Chronology of Ælfric's Works," p. 245.

Chapter Two

1. Peter Clemoes, "Ælfric," in *Continuations and Beginnings: Studies in Old English Literature.* Ed. E. G. Stanley (London, 1966), p. 182.

2. Abraham Wheloc, *Historiae Ecclesiasticae Gentis Anglorum,* Libri V. a venerabili Beda . . . Scripti. (Cambridge, 1643).

3. Kenneth Sisam, *Studies in the History of Old English Literature* (Oxford, 1953), pp. 164–65.

4. Cyril L. Smetana, "Ælfric and the Early Medieval Homiliary," *Traditio,* XV (1959), 180–81.

5. On the sources, see, in addition to Smetana, James E. Cross, "Ælfric and the Medieval Homiliary—Objection and Contribution," *Scripta Minora: Kungl. Humanistiska Vetenskapssamfundet i Lund,* 1961–1962; James E. Cross, "Bundles for Burning—A Theme in Two of Ælfric's *Catholic Homilies*—With Other Sources," *Anglia,* LXXXI (1963), 335–46; James E. Cross, "A Source for One of Ælfric's Catholic Homilies," *Englische Studien,* XXXIX (1958), 248–51; and Charles R. Davis, "Two New Sources for Ælfric's *Catholic Homilies,*" *Journal of English and Germanic Philology,* XLI (1942), 510–13. The earliest extensive studies, still valuable, are Max Förster, *Ueber die Quellen von Ælfrics Homiliae Catholicae, I: Legenden* (Berlin, 1895), and "Ueber die Quellen von Ælfrics exegetische Homiliae Catholicae," *Anglia,* XVI (1894), 1–61.

6. See Smetana, "Ælfric and the Early Medieval Homiliary," p. 180, n. 4.

7. See Note 4.

8. F. Wiegand, "Das Homiliarium Karls des Grossen auf seine ursprüngliche Gestalt hin untersucht," *Studien zur Geschichte der Theologie und der Kirche,* I (1897). Wiegand's reconstructed table of contents has been reprinted, with modifications, by J. Leclercq, "Tables pour l'inventaire des homiliaires manuscrits," *Scriptorium,* II (1948), 205–14.

9. Clemoes, "Ælfric," p. 183.

10. See Cyril L. Smetana, "Ælfric and the Homiliary of Haymo of Halberstadt," *Traditio,* XVII (1961), 457–69. (The Haymo referred to is actually Haymo of Auxerre.)

11. Enid M. Raynes, "MS Boulogne-sur-Mer 63 and Ælfric," *Medium Aevum,* XXVI (1957), 65–73.

12. For a brief introductory treatment of this subject, see Harry Caplan, "The Four Senses of Scriptural Interpretation and the Medieval Theory of Preaching," *Speculum,* IV (1929), 282–90.
13. Quoted by Caplan, p. 284.
14. See Hanspeter Schelp, "Die Deutungstradition in Ælfrics Homiliae Catholicae," *Archiv,* CXCVI (1960), 273–95.
15. Schelp, "Die Deutungstradition . . . ," p. 280.
16. See Clemoes, "Ælfric," p. 191.
17. See Smetana, "Ælfric and the Early Medieval Homiliary," p. 188.
18. Förster, *Anglia*, XVI (1894), 58.

Chapter Three

1. Peter Clemoes, "The Chronology of Ælfric's Works," in *The Anglo-Saxons: Studies in some Aspects of their History and Culture*. Ed. Peter Clemoes (London, 1959), p. 219.
2. See, however, A. A. Prins, "Some Remarks on Ælfric's *Lives of Saints* and His Translations from the Old Testament," *Neophilologus,* XXV (1940), 112–22. Prins points out that Dietrich and Maclean both arrived at the number forty, but by different means, both questionable. Prins believes the extant manuscript contains only thirty-eight items and thinks the paraphrases of Judges and Esther must have originally been part of the set.
3. "The Chronology of Ælfric's Works," p. 220.
4. See J. H. Ott, *Ueber die Quellen der Heiligenleben in Ælfrics Lives of Saints* I (Halle, 1892), and C. Grant Loomis, "Further Sources of Ælfric's Saints' Lives," *Harvard Studies and Notes in Philosophy and Literature,* XIII (1931), 1–8.
5. See Constance L. Rosenthal, *The 'Vitae Patrum' in Old and Middle English Literature* (Philadelphia, 1936).
6. The fullest and most recent treatment is T. Wolpers, *Die englische Heiligenlegende des Mittelalters* (Tübingen, 1964). Still useful are G. H. Gerould, *Saints' Legends* (Boston, 1916); C. W. Jones, *Saints' Lives and Chronicles in Early England* (Ithaca, N.Y., 1947); and Bertram Colgrave, "The Earliest Saints' Lives Written in England," *Proceedings of the British Academy,* XLIV (1958), 35–60.
7. See C. E. Wright, *The Cultivation of Saga in Anglo-Saxon England* (London, 1939), pp. 40–51.
8. Rosemary Woolf, "Saints' Lives," in *Continuations and Beginnings: Studies in Old English Literature*. Ed. E. G. Stanley (London, 1966), p. 64.
9. Clemoes, "The Chronology of Ælfric's Works," p. 222.
10. "Saints' Lives," p. 40.
11. "Saints' Lives," pp. 64–65.

12. See Woolf, "Saints' Lives," pp. 43–44.

13. Dorothy Bethurum, "The Form of Ælfric's *Lives of Saints,*" *Studies in Philology,* XXIX (1932), 522–23.

14. *An Old English Martyrology,* ed. G. Herzfeld. Early English Text Society, 116 (London, 1900).

15. See C. Grant Loomis, *White Magic* (Cambridge, Mass., 1948).

16. A good account of the Antonian life is Benjamin R. Kurtz, "From St. Antony to St. Guthlac: a study in biography," *University of California Studies in Modern Philology,* XII (1926), 104–46.

17. See Ott, *Ueber die Quellen . . . ,* p. 58.

18. G. H. Gerould, "Ælfric's Lives of St. Martin of Tours," *Journal of English and Germanic Philology,* XXIV (1925), 206–10.

19. See Ott, *Ueber die Quellen . . . ,* pp. 59–60.

20. C. Grant Loomis, "The Growth of the Saint Edmund Legend," *Harvard Studies and Notes in Philology and Literature,* XIV (1932), 83–113.

Chapter Four

1. Peter Clemoes, "The Chronology of Ælfric's Works," in *The Anglo-Saxons: Studies in some Aspects of their History and Culture.* Ed. Peter Clemoes (London, 1959), p. 240.

2. For a sound summary, see W. A. Craigie, "The English Versions (To Wyclif)," in *The Bible in Its Ancient and English Versions.* Ed. H. Wheeler Robinson (Oxford, 1940), pp. 128–45.

3. Arthur H. Abel, *Ælfric and the West-Saxon Gospels.* Unpubl. diss., University of Pennsylvania, 1962.

4. H. L. Hargrove, ed., *King Alfred's Old English Version of St. Augustine's Soliloquies.* Yale Studies in English, VIII (New Haven, 1904), p. 1.

5. W. J. Sedgefield, ed., *King Alfred's Old English Version of Boethius' De Consolatione Philosophiae* (Oxford, 1899), p. 1.

6. Quoted in Flora Ross Amos, *Early Theories of Translation* (New York, 1920), p. 55.

7. An interesting study of the way Ælfric referred to his work is Ann E. Nichols, "*Awendan:* A Note on Ælfric's Vocabulary," *Journal of English and Germanic Philology,* LXIII (1964), 7–13.

8. The most thorough study is Charles R. Davis, *Biblical Translations in Ælfric's Catholic Homilies.* Unpubl. diss., New York University, 1949. (An abridgment of this dissertation was published by N.Y.U., 1949.)

9. The subject is reviewed by Abel, *Ælfric and the West-Saxon Gospels.* (See Note 3.)

10. Davis, *Biblical Translations in Ælfric's Catholic Homilies,* abridgment, p. 6.

11. *Ibid.,* pp. 1–4. See also Max Förster, "Ælfric's s.g. Hiob-Uebersetzung," *Anglia,* XV (1893), 473–77.

12. Marguerite-Marie Dubois, *Ælfric: Sermonnaire, Docteur, et Grammairien* (Paris, 1943), p. 90.

13. Dubois, *Ælfric,* pp. 93–94.

14. The subject is reviewed and discussed in Josef Raith, "Ælfric's Share in the Old English Pentateuch," *Review of English Studies,* NS III (1952), 305–24.

15. Clemoes, "The Chronology of Ælfric's Works," p. 225.

Chapter Five

1. They are listed in the foreword to Zupitza's edition.

2. See books cited in Chapter 1, Note 23.

3. On the history of grammar, see J. E. Sandys, *A History of Classical Scholarship* I (Cambridge, 1903), 88–102.

4. A useful survey of early grammars is provided by Jackson J. Campbell, "Knowledge of Rhetorical Figures in Anglo-Saxon England," *Journal of English and Germanic Philology,* LXVI (1967), 5–10.

5. See Lawrence K. Shook, *Ælfric's Latin Grammar: A Study in Old English Grammatical Terminology.* Unpubl. diss., Harvard University, 1939, pp. 17–24.

6. *Ibid.,* pp. 20–21.

7. See, in addition to Shook, Edna R. Williams, "Ælfric's Grammatical Terminology," *Publications of the Modern Language Association,* LXXIII (1958), 453–62.

8. Marguerite-Marie Dubois, *Ælfric: Sermonnaire, Docteur et Grammairien* (Paris, 1943), p. 279.

9. They are listed in the Introduction to the best edition, G. N. Garmonsway, ed., *Ælfric's Colloquy* (London, 1939), p. 1.

10. G. N. Garmonsway, "The Development of the Colloquy," in *The Anglo-Saxons: Studies in some Aspects of their History and Culture,* ed. Peter Clemoes (London, 1959), p. 254, n. 2.

11. *Ælfric's Colloquy,* p. 10.

12. *Early Scholastic Colloquies.* Ed. W. H. Stevenson. Anecdota Oxoniensia, Medieval and Modern Series, pt. XV (Oxford, 1929). The background of the *Colloquy* has been studied by J. Zupitza, "Die ursprüngliche Gestalt von Ælfrics Colloquium," *Zeitschrift für deutsches Altertum,* XXXI (1887), 32–45; E. Schröder, "Colloquium Ælfrici," *Zeitschrift für deutsches Altertum,* XLI (1897), 283–90; and Garmonsway, "The Development of the Colloquy" (see Note 10, above).

13. "The Development of the Colloquy," pp. 258–60.

14. Eric Colledge, "An Allusion to Augustine in Ælfric's 'Colloquy,'" *Review of English Studies,* NS XII (1961), 180–81.

Chapter Six

1. R. W. Chambers, *The Continuity of English Prose from Alfred to More* (London, 1932).

2. See Charles S. Baldwin, *Medieval Rhetoric and Poetics* (New York, 1928), pp. 51–73.

3. Quoted by Baldwin, p. 65.

4. For example, see George Saintsbury, *History of English Prose Rhythm* (London, 1922), pp. 41–42.

5. G. H. Gerould, "Abbot Ælfric's Rhythmical Prose," *Modern Philology,* XXII (1925), 353–66.

6. *Ibid.,* p. 361.

7. Dorothy Bethurum, "The Form of Ælfric's *Lives of Saints,*" *Studies in Philology,* XXIX (1932), 515–33.

8. See Otto Funke, "Studien zur alliterierenden und rhythmischen Prosa in der älteren altenglischen Homiletic," *Anglia,* LXXX (1962), 9–36.

9. Angus McIntosh, "Wulfstan's Prose," *Proceedings of the British Academy,* XXXV (1949), 109–42; John C. Pope, "Introduction" to *Homilies of Ælfric.* Ed. John C. Pope. Vol. I. Early English Text Society 259 (London, 1967), pp. 105–36; Peter Clemoes, "Ælfric," in *Continuations and Beginnings: Studies in Old English Literature.* Ed. E. G. Stanley (London, 1966), pp. 176–209.

10. Peter Clemoes, "The Chronology of Ælfric's Works," in *The Anglo-Saxons: Studies in some Aspects of their History and Culture.* Ed. Peter Clemoes (London, 1959), p. 223. n. 3.

11. Clemoes, "Ælfric," p. 206.

12. Angus McIntosh, "Wulfstan's Prose," pp. 123–24.

13. I have departed here from the typography of both Thorpe and the rest of the quotations in this volume by spacing between "half-lines," in order to illustrate their structure more clearly.

14. "Wulfstan's Prose," p. 120.

15. *Homilies of Ælfric,* pp. 118–19.

16. Arthur Brandeis, *Die Alliteration in Ælfrics metrischen Homilien* (Vienna, 1897).

17. *Homilies of Ælfric,* p. 124.

18. *Homilies of Ælfric,* p. 128. The Schipper study is Jakob Schipper, *Grundriss der englischen Metrik* (Vienna, 1895), pp. 39–43.

19. Clemoes, "The Chronology of Ælfric's Works," p. 222.

20. *Homilies of Ælfric,* pp. 125–27.

Selected Bibliography

Primary Sources

Almost all of Ælfric's works have been printed, but the editions are of uneven quality and some are difficult to obtain. This situation is being partially remedied both by new editions and by the reissue of some of the older editions. The first volume of Pope's edition of the previously unprinted homilies has appeared (see below) and a new edition of *Catholic Homilies* I is being prepared by Peter Clemoes for the Early English Text Society. The principal manuscripts are listed in the *Cambridge Bibliography of English Literature*. Ed. F. W. Bateson (Cambridge, 1941), I. 89–92, and in more detail, in N. R. Ker, *Catalogue of Manuscripts Containing Anglo-Saxon* (Oxford, 1957). The following list gives the best editions currently available in the order of their publication.

The Homilies of the Anglo-Saxon Church. The First Part containing the Sermones Catholici or Homilies of Ælfric. Ed. Benjamin Thorpe. 2 volumes. London: Ælfric Society, 1844–1846. No "second part" ever appeared. A translation is provided.

The Anglo-Saxon Version of the Hexameron of St. Basil and the Saxon Remains of St. Basil's Admonitio ad Filium Spiritualem. Ed. H. W. Norman. Second edition. London: J. R. Smith, 1849. Still the only edition of the *Admonitio*, but superseded by Crawford's edition (see below) for the *Hexameron*. Translation.

"Vita S. Æthelwoldi, Episcopi Wintoniensis, Auctore Ælfrico," in *Chronicon Monasterii de Abingdon*. Ed. J. Stevenson, Rolls Series 1858, Vol. II, pp. 255–66. In Latin. No translation, but translated by S. H. Gem, *An Anglo-Saxon Abbot* (Edinburgh: T. and T. Clark, 1912), pp. 166–80.

Old English Homilies, First Series. Ed. R. Morris. Early English Text Society OS 29 and 34. London: N. Trübner, 1867–1868. Ælfric's *De XII Abusivis* appears in two versions, pp. 107–19 and 299–304. The first version is translated.

Ælfrics Grammatik und Glossar. Ed. J. Zupitza. Sammlung englischer Denkmaler in kritischen Ausgaben. Berlin: Weidmann, 1880. Reprinted Darmstadt: Wissenschaftliche Buchgesellschaft, 1967, with a new preface by H. Gneuss.

"Ælfric's Version of Alcuini Interrogationes Sigeuulfi in Genesin." Ed.

G. E. Maclean. *Anglia,* VI (1883), 425–73, and VII (1884), 1–59. No translation.

Angelsächsische Homilien und Heiligenleben, Ed. B. Assmann. Bibliothek der angelsächsischen Prosa III. Kassel: G. H. Wigand, 1889. Reprinted Darmstadt: Wissenschaftliche Buchgesellschaft, 1964, with a supplementary introduction in English by Peter Clemoes. Items I–IX are by Ælfric. No translation.

Ælfric's Lives of Saints. Ed. W. W. Skeat. Early English Text Society OS 76, 82, 94, and 114. London: N. Trübner, 1881–1900. Translation provided.

"Excerpta ex Institutionibus Monasticis Æthelwoldi Episcopi Wintoniensis Compilata in Usum Fratrum Egneshamnensium per Ælfricum Abbatem." Ed. Mary Bateson. In *Compotus Rolls of the Obedientiaries of St. Swithun's Priory, Winchester.* Ed. G. W. Kitchin. London: Hampshire, 1892, pp. 171–98. Ælfric's letter to the monks of Eynsham; no translation.

Twelfth-Century Homilies in M. S. Bodley 343. Ed. A. O. Belfour, Early English Text Society OS 137. London: Oxford University Press, 1909. Items I–IV, VII–IX, XIII and XIV are by Ælfric. Translation provided.

Texte und Untersuchungen zur altenglischen Literatur und Kirchengeschichte. Ed. Rudolf Brotanek. Halle: M. Niemeyer, 1913. Item I (pp. 3 ff.) is by Ælfric. No translation.

Die Hirtenbriefe Ælfrics. Ed. Bernhard Fehr. Bibliothek der angelsächsischen Prosa, IX. Hamburg: H. Grand, 1914. Re-issued, Darmstadt: Wissenschaftliche Buchgesellschaft, 1966, with a supplement by Peter Clemoes. Contains Ælfric's pastoral letters, both English and Latin, and two Latin tracts on the seven ecclesiastical orders and the Ten Commandments. German translation provided.

Exameron Anglice. Ed. S. J. Crawford. Bibliothek der angelsächsischen Prosa, X. Hamburg: H. Grand, 1921. English translation provided.

The Old English Version of the Heptateuch. Ed. S. J. Crawford. Early English Text Society 160. London: Oxford University Press, 1922. Also contains "On the Old and New Testaments" *(Letter to Sigeweard)* and the Preface to Genesis. Only the *Letter to Sigeweard* is translated.

Ælfric's De Temporibus Anni. Ed. H. Henel. Early English Text Society 213. London: Oxford University Press, 1942. No translation.

Ælfric's Colloquy. Ed. G. N. Garmonsway. Methuen's Old English Library. 2nd edition, London: Methuen. 1947.

Ælfric's First Series of Catholic Homilies. British Museum Royal 7C. XII, fols., 4–218. Ed. Norman Eliason and Peter Clemoes. EEMF XIII. Copenhagen: Rosenkilde and Bagger, 1966. Facsimile.

Homilies of Ælfric: A Supplementary Collection. Ed. John C. Pope. Vol. I. Early English Text Society 259. London: Oxford University Press, 1967. No translation.

SECONDARY SOURCES

I. Books

BARRETT, CHARLES R. *Studies in the Word-Order of Ælfric's Catholic Homilies and Lives of Saints.* Occasional Papers, No. III, Department of Anglo-Saxon, Cambridge University, 1953. A useful stylistic study.

DUBOIS, MARGUERITE-MARIE. *Ælfric: Sermonnaire, Docteur et Grammairien.* Paris: E. Droz, 1943. Lengthy and often useful, though not always reliable in detail.

GEM, S. H. *An Anglo-Saxon Abbot: Ælfric of Eynsham.* Edinburgh: T. and T. Clark, 1912. A popular treatment, intended to present Ælfric and his times as relevant to England on the eve of World War I. Useful mainly for its translations of the Latin works.

JOST, KARL. *Wulfstanstudien.* Schweizer anglistische Arbeiten, XXIII. Bern: 1950. Contains much useful material on Ælfric's language. See, especially, pp. 159–76.

POPE, JOHN C. "Introduction" to *Homilies of Ælfric: A Supplementary Collection.* Early English Text Society 259. London: Oxford University Press, 1967. This book is listed above, but special attention should be called to the 190-page introduction, a major contribution to Ælfric studies.

SISAM, KENNETH. *Studies in the History of Old English Literature.* Oxford: Oxford University Press, 1953. "MSS Bodley 340 and 342: Ælfric's *Catholic Homilies,*" pp. 148–98, and "The Order of Ælfric's Early Books," pp. 298–301.

WHITE, CAROLINE L. *Ælfric: A New Study of His Life and Writings.* Yale Studies in English, II. New Haven, Conn.: Yale University Press, 1898. Old, but not completely superseded. Closely based upon Dietrich (1855–1856).

II. Essays and articles

BETHURUM, DOROTHY. "The Connection of the Katherine Group with Old English Prose," *Journal of English and Germanic Philology,* XXXIV (1935), 553–64. Important study of Ælfric's influence on Middle English literature.

———. "The Form of Ælfric's *Lives of Saints,*" *Studies in Philology,* XXIX (1932), 515–33. A reply to Gerould (1925), this article finds the major inspiration of Ælfric's rhythmical prose to be Old English alliterative verse.

CLEMOES, PETER. "Ælfric." *Continuations and Beginnings: Studies in Old English Literature.* Ed. E. G. Stanley. London: Nelson, 1966, pp. 176–209. Graceful, scholarly appreciation.

———. "The Chronology of Ælfric's Works," in *The Anglo-Saxons: Studies in some Aspects of their History and Culture Presented to Bruce*

Dickins. Ed. Peter Clemoes. London: Bowes and Bowes, 1959, pp. 212–47. An indispensable guide to Ælfric's canon and its chronology.

———. "The Old English Benedictine Office, CCCC MS 190, and The Relationships Between Ælfric and Wulfstan: A Reconsideration," *Anglia,* LXXVIII (1960), 281–83. A reply to Bernhard Fehr, "Das Benediktiner-Offizium und die Beziehungen zwischen Ælfric und Wulfstan," *Englische Studien,* XLVI (1913), 338 and 344–45. Clemoes points out that there is no evidence that Ælfric made the extract from Hrabanus Maurus referred to.

CROSS, JAMES E. "Ælfric and the Medieval Homiliary—Objection and Contribution," *Scripta Minora: Kungl. Humanistiska Vetenskaps-samfundet i Lund.* 1961–1962. Supplements Smetana (1959) by pointing out several other sources for the *Catholic Homilies* in sermons found in the homiliary of Paul the Deacon.

———. "Bundles for Burning—A Theme in Two of Ælfric's Catholic Homilies—With Other Sources," *Anglia,* LXXXI (1963), 335–46. Continues the study of sources.

DIETRICH, EDWARD. "Abt Ælfrik: Zur Literatur-Geschichte der angelsächsischen Kirche," Niedner's *Zeitschrift für historische Theologie,* XXV (1855), 487–595; XXVI (1856), 163–256. The pioneer work in modern Ælfric studies; still not completely superseded.

FÖRSTER, MAX. *Ueber die Quellen von Ælfric's Homiliae Catholicae.* I: Legenden. Berlin, 1892. Still of value for the sources. The exegetical homilies are added in *Anglia,* XVI (1894), 1–61.

FUNKE, OTTO. "Some Remarks on Late Old English Word-Order with Special Reference to Ælfric and the Maldon Poem," *Englische Studien,* XXXVII (1956), 99–104. Supplements Barrett (1953).

———. "Studien zur alliterierenden und rhythmischen Prosa in der älteren altenglischen Homiletic," *Anglia,* LXXX (1962), 9–36. Good study of rhythmical styles before Ælfric.

GARMONSWAY, G. N. "The Development of the Colloquy," in *The Anglo-Saxons: Studies in some Aspects of their History and Culture Presented to Bruce Dickins.* Ed. Peter Clemoes. London: Bowes and Bowes, 1959, pp. 248–61. Supplements the useful introduction to Garmonsway's edition of the *Colloquy.*

GEROULD, GORDON H. "Abbot Ælfric's Rhythmical Prose," *Modern Philology,* XXII (1925), 353–66. Finds Ælfric's prose to be closely modeled on Latin "rhymed prose." See Bethurum (1932).

———. "Ælfric's Lives of St. Martin of Tours," *Journal of English and Germanic Philology,* XXIV (1925), 206–10. Good study of Ælfric's methods of adaptation.

HALVERSON, H. O. "Doctrinal Terms in Ælfric's Homilies," *University of Iowa Studies,* I. 1 (1932). Study of Ælfric's contribution to this area of the Old English vocabulary.

JOST, KARL. "The Legal Maxims in Ælfric's Homilies," *Englische Studien,* XXXVI (1955), 204–205. Brief but interesting note.

———. "Unechte Ælfrictexte," *Anglia,* LI (1927), 177–219. Examines Ælfric's contribution to the "Pentateuch." See Raith (1952).

KISBYE, TORBEN. "Zur pronominalen Anrede bei Ælfric," *Archiv,* CCI (1964), 423–35. Useful contribution to the study of Ælfric's style.

LADD, C. A. "The 'Rubens' Manuscript and 'Archbishop Ælfric's Vocabulary,'" *Review of English Studies,* XI (1960), 353–64. Study in attribution.

LOOMIS, C. GRANT. "Further Sources of Ælfric's Saints' Lives," *Harvard Studies and Notes in Philology and Literature,* XIII (1931), 1–8. Supplements Ott (1892).

MCINTOSH, ANGUS. "Wulfstan's Prose," Sir Israel Gollancz Memorial Lecture. *Proceedings of the British Academy,* XXXV (1949), 109–42, and separately. Also contains a precise and accurate description of Ælfric's style and a contrast of it with Wulfstan's.

MEISSNER, PAUL. "Studien zum Wortschatz Ælfrics," *Archiv,* CLXV (1934), 11–19; CLXVI (1935), 30–39. Notes on Ælfric's vocabulary.

NEEDHAM, GEOFFREY. "Additions and Alteration in Cotton MS Julius E VII," *Review of English Studies,* IX (1958), 160–64. Useful study of the principal MS of *Lives of Saints.*

NICHOLS, ANN E. "*Awendan:* A Note on Ælfric's Vocabulary," *Journal of English and Germanic Philology,* LXIII (1964), 7–13.

OTT, J. H. *Ueber die Quellen der Heiligenleben in Ælfric's Lives of Saints.* Halle, 1892. Still useful. See also Loomis (1931).

PRINS, A. A. "Some Remarks on Ælfric's *Lives of Saints* and His Translations from the Old Testament," *Neophilologus,* XXV (1940), 112–22. Considers the question of the number of items originally in *LS* and concludes that Judges and Esther, or perhaps Judith, must have once been part of the set.

RAITH, JOSEF, "Ælfric's Share in the Old English Pentateuch," *Review of English Studies,* NS III (1952), 305–24. Valuable review of the problem.

RAYNES, ENID M. "MS Boulogne-sur-Mer 63 and Ælfric," *Medium Aevum,* XXVI (1957), 65–73. Offers evidence that the MS is a "commonplace book" made by Ælfric.

SCHELP, HANSPETER, "Die Deutungstradition in Ælfrics Homiliae Catholicae," *Archiv,* CXCVI (1960), 273–95. Studies Ælfric's methods of interpretation.

SMETANA, CYRIL J. "Ælfric and the Early Medieval Homiliary," *Traditio,* XV (1959), 163–204. Demonstrates that Ælfric. in the *Catholic Homilies,* drew heavily upon a version of the Homiliary of Paul the Deacon. A very important study of Ælfric's sources and methods.

———. "Ælfric and the Homiliary of Haymo of Halberstadt," *Traditio,* XVII (1961), 457–69. Supplements Smetana (1959). The Haymo referred to is actually Haymo of Auxerre (See Pope, p. 157, n. 1).

WHITELOCK, DOROTHY, "Two Notes on Ælfric and Wulfstan," *Modern Language Review,* XXXVIII (1943), 124. The first note concerns the date of Ælfric's death.

WILLARD, RUDOLPH, "The Punctuation and Capitalization of Ælfric's Homily for the First Sunday in Lent," *Studies in English* (University of Texas), XXIX (1950), 1–32. Specialized but valuable study.

WILLIAMS, EDNA R. "Ælfric's Grammatical Terminology," *Publications of the Modern Language Association,* LXXIII (1958), 453–62. Study of Ælfric's coinages.

WOOLF, ROSEMARY. "Saints' Lives," in *Continuations and Beginnings: Studies in Old English Literature.* Ed. E. G. Stanley. London: Nelson, 1966, pp. 37–66. Places Ælfric in the tradition of Old English hagiography.

Index